Practical Logic

An Introduction to Critical Thinking

Practical Logic
An Introduction to Critical Thinking

John Patterson

The Dunmore Press

© 1989 John Patterson
© The Dunmore Press Ltd.

First published in 1989
by
The Dunmore Press Limited
PO Box 5115
Palmerston North
New Zealand

ISBN 0 86469 115 7

Text is set in Bookman 10/13

Layout by Anna Garland

Printed by The Dunmore Printing Company Limited, Palmerston North

Contents

Preview   1

Suppose that you have a hunch that there is something wrong with the reasons given in support of a policy change - How do you find out whether your hunch is correct? Or perhaps the arguments stated for an administrative decision do not quite support it. How do you work out exactly what is missing? This book is designed to sharpen up your skills in these areas, in Practical Logic.

The idea of this first chapter is to give you a preview of the main techniques used. Remember as you read through it that it is no more than a preview, and in particular that you will get plenty of practice at all of the techniques as you work through the exercises in the chapters that follow.

The best way to preview the techniques of argument analysis and appraisal is by means of some examples. So let's start with something simple:

> Although we all love to hear them singing at sunrise, starlings cost the farmers a small fortune because they eat vast quantities of grain.

The first question to ask is this: Is there any reasoning here? That is, does it say in the passage that certain statements are true *because* certain other ones are? As I am sure you can see, the passage clearly does contain some reasoning. It could be set out like this:

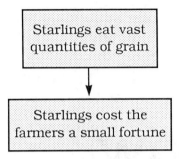

But there is another claim made: that we all love to hear them singing at sunrise. It is not so clear how that fits in with the others, so in the meantime it can be placed to one side:

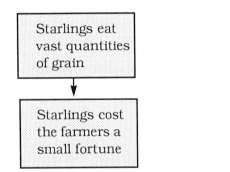

| | We all love to hear them singing at sunrise |

It is always important to ask what is the point of the whole passage. When we do that we see that we might well be meant to draw another conclusion, an unstated one: that starlings should be exterminated (or at least controlled). If that is right, then our picture of the reasoning now goes like this:

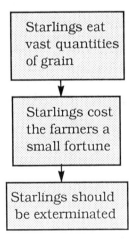

| | We all love to hear them singing at sunrise |

Remember that the first question is: *Is there any reasoning here?* Then we go on to ask the question: *What is the structure of the reasoning?* Of course we have not got very far. We have one statement sitting all alone at the side, not linked into the main pattern of reasoning. And we have been guessing about what is the main conclusion.

There are some other questions to be asked. The most important one is this: *How good are the inferences?* That is, do the conclusions follow from the reasons stated? Do they follow logically? Are the inferences *valid*, in the technical sense of this word:

> If the reasons were true, would that
> guarantee that the conclusion is true?

This is the question that you will be asking all of the time as you work through the exercises in this book. Every time you meet an inference you have to ask whether it is valid. In practice there are one or two ways of simplifying matters - in particular there is a simple test:

> Assuming the reasons to be true, is it
> possible for the conclusion to be false?

If this is possible the inference is invalid. For example (the only example we have for sure here):

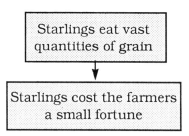

What we have to ask is, taking it as given or true that starlings do eat vast quantities of grain, could it still be false that they cost the farmers a small fortune?

When we put it this way, we see that the answer is, yes, this could well be false. Here are some conditions under which the reason could be true but the conclusion false: There is so much grain that the farmers cannot sell all that

---

they grow; Starlings eat only wild grains that the farmers do not grow.

It is a good idea to pause for a moment and try to think up some others like these. It does not matter if they are false. The point is that there are some possible conditions in which the reasons are true but the conclusion is false.

These are sometimes called *counterexamples* - examples which work against the claim that the inference is a valid one. So this inference - from the statement that they eat lots of grain to the statement that they cost the farmers a small fortune - is not valid. For it to be valid it would have to be impossible for the conclusion to be false, assuming that the reason is true.

The next task is to work out *how reliable* the inference is. We have seen that it is not entirely valid, logically. On the other hand, we have met worse inferences than this one. So, where does this one stand?

A warning - there is no simple way of answering this question. We have to make a judgment, not perform a calculation. But it is a judgment which is well worth making. And it is not difficult.

To work out how strong or reliable the inference is, ask this question:

> Assuming that the reasons are true, what is the
> probability that the conclusion is true?

The higher this probability, the stronger the inference.

In our example, we have to ask: If it were true that starlings eat vast quantities of grain, what is the probability that this would cost the farmers a small fortune? If you can work that out, you have worked out how reliable the inference is, and you do not have to be an expert to see that the probability will not be particularly high. After all, we did find some counterexamples quite easily, and they were not wildly improbable. So the inference is not a particularly reliable one.

A very useful technique for deciding the strength of an inference is to work out what would have to be added to a set of reasons for a conclusion to follow logically. Here is an example. Suppose somebody says:

> He is an accountant,
> so he is probably mean

In this inference, something is assumed. What is it? What do you have to add to the reason - "He is an accountant" - to make the conclusion follow, to make sure that he is probably mean? (I suggest that before you read on you actually commit yourself to a definite answer to this question: What *do* you have to add?)

If your answer is "All accountants are mean" you are in good company. I have had that sort of answer even from Professors of Philosophy. But it is wrong. You do not have to add that all accountants are mean for the conclusion to follow.

Perhaps you did notice that little word "probably"? Yes, you need add only that most accountants are mean, not that all of them are.

And if you feel proud of yourself for having noticed that the first time round, did you also notice the part played by another little word - "he"? The inference does not in fact require even that most accountants are mean - only that most male accountants are mean. Of course if meanness is distributed evenly amongst male and female accountants this will not make any difference in practice. But still it is a nice example of the way that the exact wording used in an inference can make a great difference to its validity.

What is the point of doing this, of working out what reasons would have to be added to guarantee the truth of the conclusion? It will help if I introduce another technical term here: If an argument is to be accepted as *sound* - as entirely satisfactory - it must satisfy two conditions:

> 1. The inferences must be valid
> 2. The reasons must be true

Of course if it satisfies both of these then the conclusion will also be true. When we use this technique of looking for *unstated reasons*, we are as it were assuming that the inferences are valid but that some of the reasons have not been stated. We find all of the unstated reasons, and then (mentally at least) add them to the stated reasons. So here:

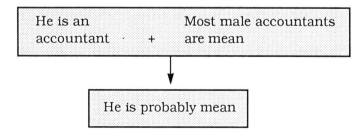

He is an accountant · + Most male accountants are mean

He is probably mean

If you have found all of the unstated reasons, then the reasoning as set out here has to be valid. And then, a useful way of assessing the original reasoning is to ask whether the reasons you have added are true. If the original reasoning cannot produce its conclusion without using some false reason, it is not acceptable reasoning.

But of course if you have added a stronger reason than you need, for the conclusion to follow, then the reason you have added will be less likely to be true. And so you may mistakenly think that the inference is worse than it actually is.

For example, it is less probable that all accountants are mean than that most of them are. If you added the stronger reason to the inference you would have judged it more harshly than it deserves.

So, you have to be careful to attend to the exact wording of the inferences you are assessing. Particularly in those cases - those frequent cases - where you know little or nothing about the subject matter.

Here is another simple example:

> I have added some blue paint to the red paint in this can, so now the paint in the can will be purple.

Those who have done a little painting will know that often the result will be a shade of red, or a shade of blue, or even brown, rather than purple.

If you did not know that, you may want to complain that you are at a disadvantage in this sort of case - "How can I be expected to know that sort of thing?" But even those who are blissfully ignorant of the interaction of pigments should be able to see (and to say) that the inference assumes, amongst other things, something like this:

> Blue plus red gives purple

We may not know that this is not always true, but we should be able to write it down.

At first though it seems to many folk so obvious that blue added to red gives purple that it just does not occur to them to write it down. But it is important to write it down, and it is important to realise that, logically speaking, anything could happen when you mix two substances. Red paint plus blue paint could produce a three course meal, or little green men. And once you fully realise this you will find that possibilities occur to you which did not occur to you before. (Which brings to mind another assumption made in the inference - that paint plus paint makes paint.)

That in a sense is what this book is all about. Not a training in computational techniques, but rather a way of improving your powers of *logical imagination.*

It is important to realise that an inference or series of inferences is usually found embedded in a long passage. And that a series of inferences can itself be very long and complex, with reasons for reasons for reasons, and reasons against reasons against, and so on. But the crucial thing is to have a very good feel for how to assess the reliability of a single inference. When you have mastered that, longer examples are fairly easy. Because, after all, a long reasoned argument is almost always a combination of several simple inferences. You can deal with the simple arguments one at a time.

So for example if you were to deal at all thoroughly with the starling example you would at least have to deal with the other inference:

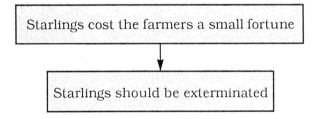

And another whole set of counterexamples would have to be considered.

Not that you often have to deal with all of the inferences in a passage, in detail. You will soon develop a good "nose" for the weak points and the interesting points. And when there is a range of techniques that might be applied to a problem - such as our two rather different-looking ways of assessing the reliability of an inference - you quickly develop skill in selecting techniques appropriate to the example in hand.

To learn how to make a really penetrating appraisal of any inference you might happen to meet, the book provides plenty of examples to practise on, with detailed model answers. It is one thing to master a chapter of an academic textbook, but the real test comes in applying it.

Above all, it is important not only to respond appropriately to a range of types of reasoning, but also to be able to *defend* your responses, to explain what you are doing and why you are doing it, ideally to somebody who has not been working through this book at all. I firmly believe that the best test of whether you really understand what is going on is whether you can explain it to an outsider.

Reasons and Conclusions 2

This chapter outlines the preliminary stages of argument analysis. When you are analysing a passage the first thing that has to be decided is what is being inferred from what, what reasons are being offered in support of what conclusions. The preliminary stages consist in *identifying* the reasons and the conclusions, in *separating* them out from any extraneous matter there may be in a passage.

Sentences and statements

Reasons and conclusions have to be statements. Thus in the accountant example, the reason given is the statement that he is an accountant, and the conclusion is the statement that he is probably mean. In the paint mixing example, the conclusion is the statement that the paint in the can will now be purple, and the reason is the statement that I have added some blue paint to the red paint in the can.

Note that in both these cases the whole argument - reason plus conclusion - can be expressed by a single sentence. It is important to realise that a sentence can express more than one statement. (And conversely, a single statement can be expressed by more than one sentence.)

An unambiguous sentence which expresses more than one statement is a *compound sentence.* Commonly, a compound sentence simply *makes* (say) two statements:

Tony cooked the dinner and Sue washed the dishes.

But a sentence can contain statements that are related in different ways. We often meet sentences which say that one statement *follows from* another one. For example:

Tony cooked the dinner and *so* Sue washed the dishes.

Here the two statements are not only *made.* The statement that Sue washed the dishes is said to be true *because* Tony cooked the dinner. The second statement is *inferred from* the first one.

Argument = reasons + inference + conclusion

We shall be using the word "argument" in a rather technical sense. In everyday speech this word suggests some sort of conflict between two parties. In logic it does not. In logic, the word "argument" applies to any case where a *conclusion* is *inferred* from *reasons.*

Look at the starling example:

> Although we all love to hear them singing at sunrise, starlings cost the farmers a small fortune because they eat vast quantities of grain.

This is an argument. A *conclusion* is *stated* - that starlings cost the farmers a small fortune. A *reason* for this conclusion is *stated* - that starlings eat vast quantities of grain. And (this is important) the conclusion is said to *follow* from the reason - "because". That is, the *conclusion* is *inferred from* the *reason.*

Good and bad reasons

At this stage we will not ask whether the reason *really does* support the conclusion. The present task is to learn how to *identify* reasons and conclusions, not how to *assess* inferences. So, when we call one statement a reason for another one, we are *not* saying that it is a *good* reason. We will worry about that later.

Thus in the accountant example - "He is an accountant, so he is probably mean" - the reason *given* for the conclusion that he is probably mean is that he is an accountant. This may be a good reason, or it may be a bad reason. But we do not have to know that to know that it is *given* as a reason. We tell that by noticing the word "so", in the passage.

Inference words

In the accountant example the word "so" functions as an *inference word.* It does the same in the paint mixing example:

> I have added some blue paint to the red paint in this can, *so* now the paint in the can will be purple.

In the starling example this function is performed by the word "because". There are a lot of other words and expressions which can be used to indicate that one statement is to be inferred from other statements: "since", "for", "hence", "which shows that", "therefore", and so on and so on.

It would be futile to try to give a complete list. Whether a word is being used as an inference word can depend upon *how* it is used. One and the same word can be used sometimes as an inference word and at other times with another function. But usually it is clear enough how it is being used, so there should not be anything much to worry about here.

Marking inference words

When a word is being used as an inference word in a passage it is a good idea to *mark* it in some special way. The method we will be using is to enclose it in *angle brackets*.

> He is an accountant <so> he is probably mean.

> I have added some blue paint to the red paint in this can, <so> now the paint in the can will be purple.

> Although we all love to hear them singing at sunrise, starlings cost the farmers a small fortune <because> they eat vast quantities of grain.

This is the *first stage of argument analysis.* It can be done directly on a passage in a newspaper or book, if you do not mind the odd pencil mark.

Marking reasons & conclusions

The *second stage* is to *mark the reasons and conclusions.* As accurately as you can, divide each reason and each conclusion from the rest of the passage with *slash marks.* And *underline* all conclusions.

> /He is an accountant/ <so> /he is probably mean/.

> /I have added some blue paint to the red paint in this can/, <so> /now the paint in the can will be purple/.

> Although we all love to hear them singing at sunrise, /starlings cost the farmers a small fortune/ <because> /they eat vast quantities of grain/.

Again you can mark directly onto the printed text.

Interpretation

It is not always easy to identify reasons and conclusions in a passage. In particular, if the passage is not very well written it may be far from clear what is being said (conclusions), and why (reasons). In such cases you should feel free to *restate* the reasons and conclusions, so that it *is* clear what is being said and why. If you find a passage to be vague, ambiguous or in any way confused or unclear, say so. Then *interpret* the passage as reasonably as you can, so as to remove the uncertainty, *restating* the reasons and conclusions clearly, as interpreted. Of course you may fail to give the *intended* interpretation, but that is not your fault. Just try to be fair, and sensitive.

Remember

REASONS AND CONCLUSIONS

Mark the inference words: < >
Mark reasons & conclusions: / /
Underline conclusions: _____
Restate unclear passages

Exercises & model answers

It is important throughout this book to start doing the exercises as soon as possible. Although there are many more points which will have to be made, I shall leave them until later, so that you can try your hand at sorting out reasons and conclusions and inference words.

You may have noticed that there are *model answers* to the exercises. These are here to be used. When you have attempted an exercise or a small group of them, look up the model answers and see how you are getting on. In particular, do this if you get stuck. *This is not cheating* - it is a perfectly legitimate way of making progress.

And please, always look at the model answers *in detail.* You will probably find differences between your answers and mine. Think about these differences - sometimes both answers will be acceptable, sometimes you will see that your answer could be improved, and sometimes your answer will be better than mine. There is also a lot of supplementary comment amongst the model answers. Indeed, many of the most important points are made there.

Finally, when answering an exercise, unless it is absolutely obvious what the answer is, your answer should be explained in a few words. *Write your explanation down.* Imagine that you are explaining it to a reasonably intelligent person who has not read this book or studied logic at all. Often points which you thought were crystal clear turn out not to be at all clear when you try explaining them. On the other hand you will find that the very process of writing down an explanation helps to make them clear.

EXERCISE 2

Mark the reasons, conclusions and inference words in the following passages.
Use slashes to mark off each /reason/ and /conclusion/.
Underline each conclusion.
Enclose <inference words> in angle brackets.
You may restate any unclear passages.
Unless it is absolutely self-explanatory, explain your answer.

201 /Bread baked from stone ground organic wholemeal flour is far better for you than white bread/<because>/it contains no harmful residues./

202 /A particle in a fluid is able to move freely in any direction./ <So>/the pressure in a fluid must be the same in every direction./

203 /Policemen walk a lot./ <That is why>/they have such large feet./

204 The fact that/the sun is slowly cooling down/<means that>/life on earth as we know it will eventually cease./

205 /The government cannot afford to admit the level of unemployment./ To do so would reveal the total inadequacy of its social and economic policies. *are totally inadequate/.* */the goverment's*

206 /Our religious and political leaders no longer command the attention and obedience of the masses,/<and><so>/we drift towards moral chaos./

207 Everyone knows that/there is no certain path to success in business./ Even/the best trained and rewarded employee can let you down,/your closest associate may renege on a deal,/and /a sudden change in government policy or in the exchange rate can turn a profitable operation into a disaster./

208 <Because>/we see them every day on television,/we know the newsreaders better than our own aunts and uncles./

209 When you are tying up a parcel for posting, get someone to hold the first half knot tight while you tie the second one. The job is not at all easy to start with, and there's nothing worse than trying to do three jobs with two hands.

210 When you write to your bank manager complaining about poor service, remember that he is a powerful person. Some day you will be wanting a favour from him, so it would be foolish to anger him unnecessarily.

211 Because of the close links between our emotions and our actions, a person whose actions are abnormal is probably suffering from some emotional disorder.

212 The enjoyment of athletics is by no means confined to able-bodied people. The thrill of competition and the wish to excel is present in every group, and this includes those who are handicapped in body or in mind. If you have lost the use of an arm you might have a little trouble with balance, but you are not prevented from running, hurdling, jumping etc; if you have lost the use of a leg you can still take part in the throwing events.

213 Genuine wrought iron is expensive, not because it is difficult to make but because there is a very small demand for it and hence the retailers are reluctant to carry stocks.

214 Educational spending is a major cause of inflation. A great deal of money is fed into the economy without a corresponding increase in productive output, and that is exactly the sort of thing which brings about inflation.

215 Prepainted roofing iron outlasts regular iron by as much as ten years. And it is expensive to replace a roof. So if you want to save in the long term you should use prepainted iron.

216 Ratings as measures of success are usually thought of as subjective since they ask for individual interpretation and judgment in the basic data, but in numerical form, they often appear to be objective. The objective measures (earnings, output, stability) involve interpretation in the decision to use such data. Thus there are really no purely objective or subjective measures of success, although it is useful at times to categorise measures in these terms.

217 Small rural road boards ought to be amalgamated. The number of administrative staff needed would thus be reduced, while a great deal of worn-out equipment would not have to be replaced and so there would be a saving of scarce overseas funds.

218 A democratically elected government is obliged to do what the people want. It follows that a government policy is justified only through the mandate granted to the government by the electors. From this I conclude that a government is not entitled to introduce policies not mentioned in its manifesto.

219 The rounded personality of the man of tomorrow requires more than mere passive spectatorship. For their physical and mental balance alike human beings need to know and practice one of the arts. Through the amateur cultural movement, lay participation is secured engendering greater appreciation and the awakening of sensibilities and gifts which channelled through the schools, may issue in major work. But this is not enough. To build a balanced personality the work must start in the very earliest stages of education. It is for this reason that an ambitious plan has been developed for the teaching of the arts at the elementary level of schooling.

220 Historically, the idea of freedom of occupational choice is comparatively new. In ancient and medieval times, a person had little freedom to choose an occupation that appealed to him. Social and occupational level and even field were determined primarily by birth.

EXERCISE TWO - MODEL ANSWERS

Exercise 201

/Bread baked from stone ground organic wholemeal flour is far better for you than white bread/ <because> /it contains no harmful residues/

Often the conclusion of an argument does come at the "conclusion" of a passage, but here it comes at the beginning. Sometimes it comes in the middle.

You may substitute for pronouns and noun phrases. If you find it clearer write out the reason fully: "Bread baked from stoneground wholemeal organic flour contains no harmful residues." I doubt if anyone would be confused by the pronoun "it" in a short passage like this one, but in some exercises this will be a useful move. There is a convention that square brackets are used around anything added to the original text. For example;

/Bread baked from stone ground organic wholemeal flour is far better for you than ordinary bread/ <because> /[bread baked from stone ground organic wholemeal flour] contains no harmful residues/.

But in a really confused passage this will be far too cumbersome - feel free to ignore the convention. After all, we are concerned primarily with the *statements* made, not the *sentences* used to make them.

Exercise 202

/A particle in a fluid is able to move freely in any direction/. <So> / the pressure in a fluid must be the same in every direction/.

Exercise 203

/Policemen walk a lot/. <That is why> /they have such large feet/.

If you are not sure whether to include phrases like "that is" within an inference word bracket, as I have done here, do not worry. It usually does not matter. But in this passage you really have no option, as "why" on its own does not look like an inference word. Compare this with "that is because", where the word "because" can stand alone as an inference word.

Exercise 204

The fact that /the sun is slowly cooling down/ <means that> /life on earth as we know it will eventually cease/.

"The fact that" is not an inference word.

Also, it is better to leave it out of the reason, as I have done. Remember that a reason has to be a complete statement. "The sun is slowly cooling down" makes a statement; "The fact that the sun is slowly cooling down" does not. If that is not obvious to you, read both of the sentences aloud, imagining that you are making a statement. It does not matter *at all* whether the "that" following "means" is included in the brackets or left outside them.

Exercise 205

/The government cannot afford to admit the level of unemployment/ [<Because>] /To do so would reveal the total inadequacy of its social and economic policies/.

It is not strictly necessary to add the inference word, as I have done. But it makes the logic of the passage clearer. Of course there are several alternatives to the one I have used: "for" and "since" would do (but not "hence").

You may have split the reason into two parts: one about the social policies and one about the economic policies. Without a context we cannot tell whether this is a good move or an unnecessary one. There is nothing to show us whether it is claimed that there are, as it were, two independent inadequacies, or whether there is just one. If in doubt, it is better to split up the reasons too finely rather than not enough. So if your answer did split up the reasons, it is better than mine.

Exercise 206

/Our religious and political leaders no longer command the attention and obedience of the masses/, <and so> /we drift towards moral chaos/.

Alternatively: ". . . masses/, and <so> / . . ."

Exercise 207

Everyone knows that /there is no certain path to success in business/ [<For>] /Even the best trained and rewarded employee can let you down/, /your closest associate may renege on a deal/, and /a sudden change in government policy or in the exchange rate can turn a profitable operation into a disaster/.

Do *not* include the words "everyone knows that" in the conclusion. The reasons given are reasons for believing that there *is* no certain path to success, not for believing that everyone knows this. For that conclusion, we would need totally different reasons.

Exercise 208

<Because> /we see them every day on television/, /we know the newsreaders better than our own aunts and uncles/.

Exercise 209

/When you are tying up a parcel for posting, get someone to hold the first half knot tight while you tie the second one/. [<For>] /The job is not at all easy/ to start with, and /there's nothing worse than trying to do three jobs with two hands/.

Not such an easy one? If you are not sure what is the conclusion and what are the reasons, do not despair. It may not be your fault. And in this case I think it is fair to say that this is not entirely clear. So if your answer is not the same as mine, it may still be quite all right.

It is important not to try to get two statements from a sentence like the first one in this passage. You will get into a dreadful mess. The same goes for "If P then Q" sentences. These are *conditional*: neither part is *stated*, so neither part can be a reason or a conclusion in the argument (unless it is stated independently, somewhere else in the argument).

For example compare these sentences:

1. If John is here then we will have to go home
2. John is here and so we will have to go home.

The second one contains an argument. It *says* that John is here and *draws the inference* that we will have to go home. The first sentence does neither of these. It only says that *if* John is here *then* we will have to go home. It does not *say* that he is here. Nor does it say that we will have to go home.

So, when you come across this sort of sentence, ask whether the parts of it are being *independently stated*. If so, break it up. But if not, if all that is being stated is a *conditional relation*, do not break it up. And you cannot go by the grammar alone; sometimes a conditional sentence is used to state both a reason and a conclusion.

Exercise 210

> When you write to your bank manager complaining about poor service, remember that /he is a powerful person/. /Some day you will be wanting a favour from him/, <so> /it would be foolish to anger him unnecessarily/.

The first part of this passage can be treated as introductory. It could equally well simply be included in the first reason. But do *not* try to mark it off as an *independent* reason. It is not one. It is not part of the argument, but simply sets the scene.

In fact if part of a passage is not part of the argument, you might like to *cross it out.*

Exercise 211

> <Because> /[there are] close links between our emotions and our
> actions/, /a person whose actions are abnormal is probably suffering
> from some emotional disorder/.

This one is just a little tricky. If you mark the printed text without making any
changes, the reason is not quite *stated.* That is why I have added the words
"there are", which turn it into a complete statement. As is so often the case
there are several alternatives to the answer I have given here.

Exercise 212

> /The enjoyment of athletics is by no means confined to able-bodied
> people/. [<For>] /The thrill of competition and the wish to excel is
> present in every group, and this includes those who are handicapped
> in body or in mind/. /If you have lost the use of an arm you might have
> a little trouble with balance, but you are not prevented from running,
> hurdling, jumping etc; if you have lost the use of a leg you can still take
> part in the throwing events/.

You may well have divided up the reasons more than I have. Do not worry
about it at this stage. Later, when we are working out how *good* the argument
is, we may find that these reasons are better divided up, or better left as in my
answer.

Exercise 213

> /Genuine wrought iron is expensive/, not because it is difficult to
> make but <because> /there is a very small demand for it/ and <hence>
> /the retailers are reluctant to carry stocks/.

There are two complications here. First, the statement that genuine wrought
iron is not difficult to make does not really form part of the *argument.* So the
best thing to do is leave it out. Second, there are *two* conclusions. This is not
at all uncommon. If you are puzzled, it might help to *rewrite* the argument:

> /There is a very small demand for genuine wrought iron/ and <so> /
> the retailers are reluctant to carry stocks/. <Hence> /it is expensive/.

Exercise 214

/<u>Educational spending is a major cause of inflation</u>/. [<For>] /A great deal of money is fed into the economy without a corresponding increase in productive output/, and /that is exactly the sort of thing which brings about inflation/.

Some people get sidetracked into questions of higher economic theory by this one. So I take the opportunity of pointing out that you should resist getting upset by examples which argue for conclusions which you think are not *true*. The present job is simply to *identify* the conclusions and reasons. Do not worry about the facts of the matter.

Exercise 215

/Prepainted roofing iron outlasts regular iron by as much as ten years/And /it is expensive to replace a roof/. <So> /<u>if you want to save in the long term you should use prepainted iron</u>/.

That is a perfectly reasonable way to mark the passage. Here is another way:

/Prepainted roofing iron outlasts regular iron by as much as ten years/And /it is expensive to replace a roof/. <So> if /you want to save in the long term/ /<u>you should use prepainted iron</u>/.

Admittedly, this departs from the *wording* of the passage - all that is *said* is that *if* you want to save you should use prepainted iron. But if I met this passage outside of a logic book I would take it to be telling me to *use* prepainted iron, unconditionally. By dividing up the *conditional* sentence - which would often be a mistake - I have isolated what I think is the likely *intended* conclusion.

Note the importance of explaining what is going on. Without the explanation the second "answer" looks like a silly mistake - breaking the "rule" about not splitting conditionals.

Exercise 216

Ratings as measures of success are usually thought of as subjective since they ask for individual interpretation and judgment in the basic data, but in numerical form, they often appear to be objective. /The objective measures (earnings, output, stability) involve interpretation in the decision to use such data/. <Thus> /<u>there are really no purely objective or subjective measures of success</u>/, although it is useful at times to categorise measures in these terms.

This is a typical passage from a textbook. Someone who knows what it is all about may be able to include rather more of the passage amongst the reasons and conclusions than I have done. If you really do not know what is going on, you should look first for what seems to be the *major* conclusion, and then see what is offered in support of that.

And *if in doubt, leave it out.* That is what I have done here.

Exercise 217

/Small rural road boards ought to be amalgamated/. [<For>] /The number of administrative staff needed would thus be reduced/, while /a great deal of worn-out equipment would not have to be replaced/ and <so> /there would be a saving of scarce overseas funds/.

Here there are two conclusions. Underline both of them. And note that in this passage the word "thus" is *not* an inference word. If that is not obvious to you, try *rewriting* the statement in which it appears: "Amalgamating small rural road boards would reduce the number of administrative staff needed." This a simple statement of cause and effect, not a case of inferring a conclusion from a reason.

Exercise 218

/A democratically elected government is obliged to do what the people want/. <It follows that> /a government policy is justified only through the mandate granted to the government by the electors/. From this <I conclude that> /a government is not entitled to introduce policies not mentioned in its manifesto/.

Exercise 219

The rounded personality of the man of tomorrow requires more than mere passive spectatorship. For their physical and mental balance alike human beings need to know and practise one of the arts. Through the amateur cultural movement, lay participation is secured engendering greater appreciation and the awakening of sensibilities and gifts which channelled through the schools, may issue in major work. But this is not enough. /To build a balanced personality the work must start in the very earliest stages of education/. <It is for this reason that> /an ambitious plan has been developed for the teaching of the arts at the elementary level of schooling/.

I have treated the opening sentences as just that - opening sentences. They give some background, but as I read the passage no *arguing* takes place until we get to the end of the passage.

It is this sort of feature which tends to make it hard to deal with long passages. Look for what seems to be the *central* argument, and get that marked off. (Often it helps if you write it out clearly in your own words.) Then look at the rest of the passage. Sometimes it can all be ignored, more or less safely. Anyway, make sure that you read through the *whole* of any passage before you start working on it.

Exercise 220

/Historically, the idea of freedom of occupational choice is comparatively new/. [<For>] /In ancient and medieval times, a person had
little freedom to choose an occupation that appealed to him/. [<For>]
/Social and occupational level and even field were determined primarily by birth/.

If you marked this passage with only one conclusion - the first statement - that is acceptable. It is often not easy to tell whether a reason is itself an interme-diate conclusion or whether it stands alone.

Logical
Structure   3

Structure diagrams

It is useful to have a way of representing the *structure* of an argument in a diagram. We already have a method of marking the reasons, the conclusions, and the inference words:

/He is an accountant/ <so> /he is probably mean/.

To represent the structure in a *diagram* we first add *numbers* to the reasons and the conclusions:

1/He is an accountant/ <so> 2/he is probably mean/.

Now we can let the numbers *stand for* the reasons and conclusions, and use an *arrow* to represent the inference:

That is the basic tool we will be using from now on. It is called a structure diagram.

Chain arguments

Here is a development of the accountant example:

He is an accountant so he is probably mean - he will not lend you anything.

Marking as before, using numbers:

> 1/He is an accountant/ <so> 2/he is probably mean/ - [<therefore>]
> 3/he will not lend you anything/.

I have added another inference word in square brackets, as the third statement is clearly being inferred from the second one. The structure diagram goes like this:

This shows 2 as inferred from 1, and 3 as inferred in turn from 2. This is called a *chain argument*.

You will notice that when marking the passage I underlined both 2 and 3. Both of them are conclusions. 2 is an *intermediate* conclusion; 3 is the *final* conclusion. Thus 2 is both a reason and a conclusion: a conclusion in the inference from 1 to 2 and a reason in the inference from 2 to 3.

A final technical term: 1 is a reason which is not supported by any other reason in the passage - it is a *basic* reason (in this argument).

This can all be summarised in a diagram:

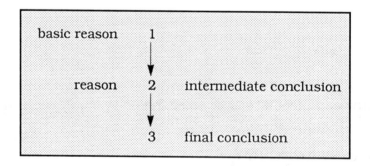

Unstated conclusions

Quite often the final conclusion of an argument is not *stated*. If you think that this has happened you should *add* what you think is the final conclusion.

For example, if we were wondering whether to ask someone for a donation to a charity, and the accountant argument (first version) arose in that context, it would be reasonable to draw the conclusion that it would be a waste of time to ask him:

It would be a waste of time to ask him

Another way of showing what is going on is to add the omitted conclusion to the passage, number it, and diagram in the usual way:

1/He is an accountant/ <so> 2/he is probably mean/ [<therefore> 3/ it would be a waste of time to ask him/].

And the diagram is simply this:

Linked reasons

There is another important argument structure:

Let Susan sit in the front seat. If she sits in the back she will be sick, and we do not want a mess in the car

Marking the passage and adding numbers:

1/Let Susan sit in the front seat/. [<Because>] 2/If she sits in the back she will be sick/, and 3/we do not want a mess in the car/

Here there are *two* reasons for conclusion 1, and they work in *conjunction*, not in a chain as before. This is how we represent the structure:

The plus sign and the horizontal line show that the two reasons 2 and 3 are acting together, supporting the conclusion 1. It is the *combination* of 2 and 3 that supports 1 - they are not doing this *independently* of one another.

Convergent inferences

Compare that argument with this one:

> Let Susan sit in the front seat. If she sits in the back she will be sick, and anyway it is her turn.

It is marked in much the same way as the other:

> 1/Let Susan sit in the front seat/. [<Because>] 2/If she sits in the back she will be sick/, and anyway 3/it is her turn./

But when we come to make a diagram, we see that this time the two reasons do not work in conjunction. Here we have two independent reasons for letting her sit in the front. Even if we come to reject one of them, we have to account for the other. (In the previous case this is not so.) We could represent this with two separate diagrams:

There is no plus sign and no horizontal line. Each of the reasons is linked *directly* and *independently* to the conclusion.

What we will in fact do though is join the left-hand "1" to the right-hand "1", to represent both arguments in a single diagram:

Handwriting and typing and printing

All of the methods of marking passages and representing argument structures used in this book are designed to be easily used both when writing by hand and when using a standard computer keyboard. When writing by hand you can *angle* the vertical lines so that both of them point directly to a single "1", which is not an easy task on a standard keyboard.

Likewise, the method of marking a passage is designed for handwriting, in particular so that you can work directly onto a printed text. The only difference is that when doing it by hand you should put the numbers *above* the line of text, immediately before the slash:

. . . anyway [3]/it's her turn

Linked or convergent?

Often it is not easy to decide whether an argument is linked or convergent. Of course you will try to apply the simple question:

> Are the reasons independent of one another?

The trouble is that sometimes it is not clear from the wording of the passage whether the reasons are independent.

> When in doubt, represent the
> structure as linked, not convergent.

If a reason is intended to stand on its own it is reasonable to expect some sign of this in the text. If there is no such sign, it is unreasonable to expect it to stand alone. This simple "rule" will solve a host of problems in the exercises, and usually the solution will be a reasonable one. But do not apply it indiscriminately or unthinkingly, or you will sometimes ignore important differences.

EXERCISE THREE

Mark the reasons, conclusions and inference words in these passages.
Number the reasons and conclusions.
Construct a structure diagram which represents the logical structure.
Explain why you have done what you have done.

301 I have tossed this coin ten times and it came up "heads" only once, so it is almost certain to come up "heads" next time I toss it.

302 We must stay a little longer. If we leave now we will offend your parents and we cannot afford to do that.

303 Recent research strongly indicates that the fluorocarbons used as propellants in some aerosols destroy the ozone in the upper atmosphere. Since the ozone layer protects the Earth from harmful radiation, urgent steps must be taken to ban the use of these propellants.

304 The kiwi cannot fly, having evolved in conditions where flying was not needed and where a heavy body was an advantage in digging deep for food. So over the years a series of heavier and heavier birds evolved with smaller and smaller wings, until the power of flight was lost completely.

305 You must keep off the ice, because someone broke through yesterday and so it is dangerously thin.

306 Even a very short vacation can be good for you, because it gives you a complete break from work. If you do not get away you end up a slave.

307 Do not lend your motorbike to Bill. Last time he rode one he crashed it, and anyway he's supposed to be mowing the lawns.

308 I have been trying to fix the lawnmower all morning and now it is worse than it was when I started, so I might as well give up and use it as it is, if I can.

309 When you raise the centreboard you reduce the yacht's lateral resistance, and one of the major heeling forces is provided by lateral resistance, so the yacht is less likely to capsize if you raise the centreboard.

310 You may have heard about mulching the garden. This is good in the spring because the mulch helps keep the soil moist in the summertime, and at the same time it prevents most weeds from germinating.

311 Your car is ready for the junk yard, Tom. You can see the rust from the other side of the carpark, and the engine sounds dreadful.

312 Our hospitals are so full of drink-drive accident cases that you have to wait months and months for a simple operation. That is not good enough - we must do something to reduce the number of drinking drivers. The blood alcohol limit will have to be reduced - to zero.

313 If you drive with your foot resting lightly on the clutch pedal the clutch will wear out because the plates will be rubbing against each other.

314 Medical care is, paradoxically, one of the major threats to the human species. Now that the major contagious diseases have been conquered, medical science will soon find effective cures for the degenerative diseases. When this happens, life expectancy will increase dramatically, food and housing resources will consequently become so inadequate that a major social breakdown will be inevitable.

315 You have been driving with your foot resting against the clutch pedal and so the plates have been rubbing against each other. That is why the clutch is worn out.

316 It is a good idea to signal your intentions well before you turn. In the first place you are more likely to find out what other drivers are going to do because they will follow your example. But more importantly, if you develop this habit you will learn to make up your mind earlier, and that will make you a better driver, as you will be less likely to act impulsively.

317 Plant your vegetables in straight rows running north-south. That way you can keep them weeded and the sun can get to all of the plants.

318 Mary was alone in the house when she went to bed and when she is alone she always leaves the hall light on, so it should still have been on when Dave got home. But he swears it was off. That means somebody else must have turned it off.

319 The University system is in chaos. Both the Government and the University authorities are more concerned with holding on to power than with providing a good education for our young people. And the academics are no better. The only solution is to let the students take over.

320 One of the advantages of a folding kayak is that you can handle it entirely on your own. Then there is the sheer simplicity of it - just a few sticks and some canvas, plus a paddle. More practically Susan, your back is past its best, so you want a really light boat. All this means that you would find a folding kayak much more relaxing than some big heavy motorboat. And it would suit me better too - there would be enough money left over for that trip to Switzerland. So that's what you should get - an old fashioned folding kayak, not a smelly motorboat.

321 The old-fashioned method of designing a boat by making a solid wooden half-model and shaving off tiny pieces until it looks just right will no longer produce competitive yachts. A professional designer can eliminate hundreds of major variations by computer analysis and tank testing, so he has a formidable advantage over the traditional designer-builder.

322 Many species of wetlands birdlife face extinction. With the spread of agriculture and increased urbanisation both their habitat and their very lives are threatened. Swamps are drained for new pasture land and agricultural pesticides kill off the insects upon which many birds depend, directly or indirectly. Moreover, since wetland birds tend to be poor fliers and nest at ground level, they are easy prey for domestic cats, and so with every new suburb, vast numbers are killed off.

323 We must stay a little longer. If we leave now we will offend your parents, and anyway the supper will be served soon and I am starving.

324 Do not wear your high-heeled shoes to the circus, Anna. Remember that time you twisted your ankle and could not walk for three days. They have those same dangerous walkways at the circus. And if you snap off a heel you will have nothing to wear on Saturday night. Anyway it would look ridiculous - everyone else will be dressed casually.

325 There is little point in saving money anymore. If you are trying to survive on an ordinary salary - and few of us have any other resources - by the time you have paid your rent and bills there is very little left, so that it would take you years and years to save up even for a car, let alone a house. And with inflation, by that time what you have saved will be worth next to nothing.

326 I have never been able to understand why anyone buys a brand-new car. As I figure it out, they just are not worth the extra cost. A two-year-old car costs on the average no more than half the price of a new model. And major trouble is most unlikely in the first five years. That means you should get three good years' running for half the price of five. And there is this: about one car in twenty gives a lot of trouble right from the start. By the time it is two years old all that should have been sorted out for you.

327 Anna must have a very strong reason for throwing in her job. At her age you do not give up a good career in head office and vanish to some tiny country town. And nothing we can say will persuade her to come back, which suggests that somebody or something at head office was making her life intolerable.

328 Look, Tony, if you plant a tree so close to the house there will be all sorts of trouble in the next few years. The main drains are just a few metres away and the roots will get in and block them. That is very expensive to get fixed. Then you have to think about the leaves: if it is an evergreen it will shade the living room in winter, and that will not be very popular with Susan, and if it is deciduous the fallen leaves will block the gutters and mess up the yard.

329 Statistical studies establish beyond doubt that drink is to blame for most of our serious road accidents. We must make sure that nobody who has been drinking gets behind the wheel of a car. Our medical system cannot cope with the flood of accident cases - drunken driving must be stamped out.

330 Mother is upset, Harry - you have made another of those ugly water stains on the table. How many times do I have to tell you to use a saucer when you have a cup of coffee? It is very expensive getting the furniture repolished and we just cannot afford to do it again. It looks terrible too - imagine what people must think when they see ugly stains everywhere. And what an awful example you are setting to your little sister. I think that upsets Mother as much as the damage done to the furniture.

331 The engine is starting to give off a lot of smoke, and so it cannot be going to last much longer. This means we are not going to make it back home in the car. What is more, the leak in the radiator is getting worse, so the engine will overheat badly, especially on hills, and remember it is uphill most of the way home. So again, the car is not going to get us back. Clearly then, if we want to get home at all we will have to leave the car behind and go by bus, so we should book our seats right now.

332 It is an absolute disgrace the way grown men are appearing in public in short trousers. There should be a law banning them anywhere except the beach. Why should we have to look at ugly hairy knees in the streets and the shops? It is an aesthetic assault, and we are entitled to protection. Think of the example they set for the young! No wonder they take drugs and dye their hair if their elders and betters do not bother to dress properly! If these men want to complain that long trousers are uncomfortably hot, all I can say is that they were good enough for better men than they - a little discomfort is good for the character!

333 If you buy an ice cream then Jenny will want to have one too, and you know she is not allowed to eat anything with sugar in it - the doctor says she has diabetes. The trouble is she does not realise how serious it is and there will be a terrible fuss if she sees you with something she is not allowed to have.

334 You really should turn off that radio, Tom. You must know that it annoys the old lady next door. She needs to rest in the afternoon and if she cannot get to sleep it upsets her digestion for days. Anyway you should be working not listening to the radio. Your exams start in three days and you know you have hardly done any work since the summer.

335 When you get back from your trip to Korea I want you to give an illustrated talk to the Travel Club. They have never had anything about Korea. So what say you use transparency film rather than colour print film in your camera? That way you can put together a show where everyone can see what you are talking about. And if they are any good you should be able to sell them to an agent or publisher - they much prefer transparencies as they give much better quality reproductions.

336 You must be tired, what with the party last night and all that work in the garden today. Why not go to bed early? You need to be up at the crack of dawn tomorrow. Remember your flight to Sydney leaves at nine in the morning and you want to be in good shape when you get there, or you will have no chance of getting the job.

337 All civilised countries have banned corporal punishment in schools. It is high time we followed suit. The practice is thoroughly discredited as damaging for students and teachers alike: bad for teachers because it encourages them to become tyrannical and sadistic, and a good teacher must be exactly the opposite; bad for the pupils because it is degrading. Unless they are treated like adults rather than performing animals they will never learn to conduct themselves with maturity and dignity. The other problem with corporal punishment is that it does not work.

Indeed, the worst trouble-makers amongst the pupils take advantage of it as a means of drawing further attention to themselves.

338 I vote we eat out tonight. There is nothing in the fridge so if we are going to cook our own we will have to go shopping, and the car is not going so that would mean carrying it all back home and I am far too tired for that. And listen, there is this new fish restaurant they are all talking about. Jan went there last week and had a whole fish done that spicy Szechwan way - your favourite.

339 We really should help Aunt Jean tidy up her garden this weekend. It has become such a mess that the neighbours are complaining it spoils the street, and we do not want to upset that Mr Jones over the road - after all he is our bank manager. And remember, she is fairly well off. Who knows, she may leave some of it to us, and then we will be able to pay off the mortgage and so you can get that new car. Anyway, even if she gives it all to a cats' home, we still should give her a hand - after all she is your poor mother's only sister.

340 David is simply hopeless at playing the violin. His wrist is not supple enough and his fingers are too short, so he cannot reach the strings properly, and anyway his ear is not anywhere near good enough to play it in tune. So he should give up the violin and switch to the flute. That would be easier to live with. Nobody can make a really horrible noise on a flute, not even David. And we would not have to buy him a new instrument. Remember that his violin is in very poor condition, but he could use Mary's flute which is as good as new.

EXERCISE THREE - MODEL ANSWERS

Exercise 301

1/I have tossed this coin ten times/ and 2/it came up "heads" only once/, <so> 3/<u>it is almost certain to come up "heads" next time I toss it</u>/.

This is a simple example of linked reasoning, and the structure is made clear by the inference word "so".

Exercise 302

1/We must stay a little longer/. [<Because>] 2/If we leave now we will offend your parents/ and 3/we cannot afford to do that/.

Soon I am going to stop adding inference words, and you may be ready to do so as well. Add them if you find it helps; do not bother if you can manage without.

I hope that by now I do not have to remind you not to split up "If ... then ..." sentences except in very special circumstances.

Exercise 303

Recent research strongly indicates that 1/the fluorocarbons used as propellants in some aerosols destroy the ozone in the upper atmosphere/. <Since> 2/the ozone layer protects the Earth from harmful radiation/, 3/urgent steps must be taken to ban the use of these propellants/.

It is sometimes not easy to know whether to include phrases like the opening one in this passage or whether to leave them out. If there is any doubt they are better left out. Then you have a clear statement about, in this case, what fluorocarbons do to the atmosphere, rather than a statement about what recent research shows. If you include the opening phrase you have a completely different argument. And it would be odd to argue from those reasons to the stated conclusion.

Exercise 304

1/The kiwi cannot fly/, having 2/[It] evolved in conditions where flying was not needed and where a heavy body was an advantage in digging deep for food/. <So> 3/over the years a series of heavier and heavier birds evolved with smaller and smaller wings, until the power of flight was lost completely/.

It would be reasonable to mark "having" as an inference word, and also reasonable to split number 3.

Note the word "so" before statement 3. Without it the structure might be different, but it is there and should not be ignored.

Exercise 305

> 1/You must keep off the ice/, <because> 2/someone broke through yesterday/ <and so> 3/it is dangerously thin/.

Be careful to attend to what the passage *says.* There is a temptation to diagram this as a chain from 3 to 2 to 1, if you think that the reason why someone broke through would be that the ice is dangerously thin. That may indeed *be* the reason, but what the passage *says* is the opposite: Someone broke through yesterday *and so* the ice is dangerously thin. Read carefully. In the words of the seventeenth century poet William Walker:

> Learn to read slow: all other graces
> Will follow in their proper places.

Exercise 306

> 1/Even a very short vacation can be good for you/, <because> 2/it gives you a complete break from work/. 3/If you do not get away you end up a slave/.

This is clearly linked rather than convergent. Neither 2 nor 3 is, on its own, anything like a reason for 1. They operate together.

Exercise 307

1/Do not lend your motorbike to Bill/. 2/Last time he rode one he crashed it/, and anyway 3/he's supposed to be mowing the lawns/.

If you like you can change the conclusion from an imperative mood sentence (issuing an instruction) to an indicative mood sentence (making a statement).

Exercise 307 is definitely convergent. Compare it with this:

Do not lend your motorbike to Bill. Last time he rode one he crashed it, and you need yours to get to work.

Here the reasons reinforce each other. In the exercise you have just done they do not.

Exercise 308

1/I have been trying to fix the lawnmower all morning and now it is worse than it was when I started/, <so> 2/I might as well give up and use it as it is, if I can/.

You could if you like split 1, but I think that the first part is there to set the scene rather than to give a reason. That is, 1 starts at "now it is worse", really. And the last three words could as well be left out of the conclusion, being more in the nature of a rhetorical flourish.

Exercise 309

1/When you raise the centreboard you reduce the yacht's lateral resistance/, and 2/one of the major heeling forces is provided by lateral resistance/, <so> 3/<u>the yacht is less likely to capsize if you raise the centreboard</u>/.

If you do not know anything about naval architecture this may mean little to you. But even so I think that you should be able to work out that it is a linked argument rather than a convergent argument. As long as you know what heeling and capsizing are - and both words are in my dictionary - you should be able to work out that the two reasons are working together, not independently, even if you have no idea what lateral resistance is and would not know a centreboard from a topping lift.

Exercise 310

You may have heard about mulching the garden. 1/<u>This is good in the spring</u>/ <because> 2/the mulch helps keep the soil moist in the summertime/, and at the same time 3/it prevents most weeds from germinating/.

I have diagrammed this as convergent because each reason seems to be a sufficient reason for the conclusion. Anyway that is what you have to ask yourself, when deciding how to do the diagram. And of course if you know next to nothing about gardening, you may get it wrong. Indeed you may get it wrong even if you know quite a lot about gardening.

Exercise 311

1/<u>Your car is ready for the junk yard, Tom</u>/. 2/You can see the rust from the other side of the carpark/, and 3/the engine sounds dreadful/.

Is the passage saying that the car should be scrapped because of the rust, *and* that the car should be scrapped because of the engine? Or is it saying that the car should be scrapped because of the rust-and-the-engine? I have interpreted it the first way - as a convergent argument, in which the reasons are independent. This is because either reason, on its own, seems to support the conclusion.

But this may simply reflect my attitude to cars; certainly the passage does not force this reading. If you interpret it the second way you should diagram it as linked. And of course the *explanation* of the answer you give should make it clear why you have done what you have done. For example, if you think that a rusty car is all right as long as the engine is up to scratch, and that a car with a worn out engine is worth hanging on to provided it is not rusty - and that this seems to you to be implicit in the passage, then you will choose a linked structure - for those reasons. Finally, if you think that a passage really is ambiguous in respect of structure, you should say so - and why. I believe that this one is - that either structure is possible, that neither is ruled out.

Exercise 312

1/Our hospitals are so full of drink-drive accident cases that you have to wait months and months for a simple operation/. 2/That is not good enough - we must do something to reduce the number of drinking drivers/. 3/The blood alcohol limit will have to be reduced - to zero/.

You will notice that I have stopped underlining intermediate conclusions. If you feel you can manage as well without this prop, do so. After all, you are *saying* what you take to be the conclusions - intermediate and final - when you construct your arrow diagram.

If you divided 2 into two statements, and extended the diagram into a four-link chain, that is perfectly reasonable. Indeed, it is probably better.

Exercise 313

1/If you drive with your foot resting lightly on the clutch pedal the clutch will wear out/ <because> 2/[if you drive with your foot resting against the clutch pedal] the plates will be rubbing against each other/.

2
↓
1

Comments - after 315.

Exercise 314

1/Medical care is, paradoxically, one of the major threats to the human species/. <Now that> 2/the major contagious diseases have been conquered/. 3/medical science will soon find effective cures for the degenerative diseases/. When this happens, 4/life expectancy will increase dramatically/, 5/food and housing resources will <consequently> become so inadequate/ that 6/a major social breakdown will be inevitable/.

2
↓
3
↓
4
↓
5
↓
6
↓
1

It is not easy to mark all of the inference words. In particular, if you enclosed "when this happens" in angle brackets I will not argue with you. Nor will I if you did not separate 2 and 3 as I have done, but instead marked the whole second sentence in the passage as a single reason. Still, I think my method is a good one.

And do not worry for too long about exactly where to put the slashes which separate the parts of the passage. Sometimes the construction of the sentences makes this very difficult to do at all clearly. If you think you can make it clearer by *changing the wording*, do so. After all, what matters is *what* is said, not precisely *how* it is said.

Exercise 315

1/You have been driving with your foot resting against the clutch pedal/ <and so> 2/the plates have been rubbing against each other/ <That is why> 3/the clutch is worn out/.

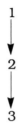

The main difference 313 and 315 is that in the second passage it is *stated* that you have been driving with your foot resting against the clutch pedal, and it is *stated* that the clutch is worn out. In the first passage neither of these is stated. It is all *conditional*. It would be a mistake to divide up the "If ... then ..." sentence. And to make the structure clear, I added the words in square brackets in 313.

Exercise 316

1/It is a good idea to signal your intentions well before you turn/. <In the first place> 2/you are more likely to find out what other drivers are going to do/ <because> 3/they will follow your example/. But more importantly, 4/if you develop this habit you will learn to make up your mind earlier/, and 5/that will make you a better driver/, <as> 6/you will be less likely to act impulsively/.

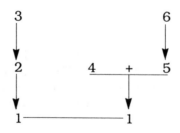

I trust that you are no longer tempted to split up the "If-then" conditional statement.

It is quite acceptable here to mark the expression "but more importantly" as an inference word.

Exercise 317

1/Plant your vegetables in straight rows running north-south/. <That way> 2/you can keep them weeded/ and 3/the sun can get to all of the plants/.

I was tempted to diagram this as convergent. Then I realised that although 2 is a reason for planting them in straight rows, as far as weeding is concerned the orientation of the rows does not matter. It is to allow the sun to get to all of the plants that you should line them up in a north-south direction (I think). So I diagrammed it as linked.

Exercise 318

1/Mary was alone in the house when she went to bed/ and 2/when she is alone she always leaves the hall light on/, <so> 3/it should still have been on when Dave got home/. But 4/he swears it was off/. <That means> 5/somebody else must have turned it off/.

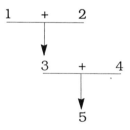

Exercise 319

1/The university system is in chaos/. 2/Both the Government and the University authorities are more concerned with holding on to power than with providing a good education for our young people. And the academics are no better/. 3/The only solution is to let the students take over/.

There is nothing wrong with dividing 2 into two or three pieces. But there in no particular advantage either, at this stage, unless you like to get practice in drawing more complicated pictures.

I want to be firm about the *order* of 1 and 3 in the diagram. The passage says the students should take over *because* the system is in chaos, even though no inference words are used.

Exercise 320

1/One of the advantages of a folding kayak is that you can handle it entirely on your own/. Then 2/there is the sheer simplicity of it - just a few sticks and some canvas, plus a paddle/. 3/More practically Susan, your back is past its best/, <so> 4/you want a really light boat/. <All this means that> 5/you would find a folding kayak much more relaxing than some big heavy motorboat/. And 6/it would suit me better too/ - 7/there would be enough money left over for that trip to Switzerland/<So> 8/that's what you should get - an old fashioned folding kayak, not a smelly motorboat/.

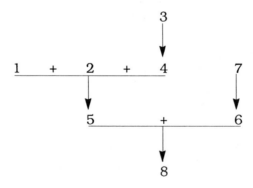

A complicated diagram, but not a difficult one to construct, as the structure of the passage is clarified with plenty of inference words.

Hint: draw the diagram from the bottom up, not from the top down.

Exercise 321

1/The old-fashioned method of designing a boat by making a solid wooden half-model and shaving off tiny pieces until it looks just right will no longer produce competitive yachts/. 2/A professional designer can eliminate hundreds of major variations by computer analysis and tank testing/, <so> 3/he has a formidable advantage over the traditional designer-builder/.

Although in the passage 2 is linked very directly to 3 by the inference word "so", 3 mentions not only the professional designer mentioned in 2 but also the traditional designer-builder mentioned in 1, and so I have diagrammed the reasoning as linked rather than convergent.

Exercise 322

1/Many species of wetlands birdlife face extinction/. 2/With the spread of agriculture and increased urbanisation both their habitat and their very lives are threatened/. 3/Swamps are drained for new pasture land/ and 4/agricultural pesticides kill off the insects upon which many birds depend, directly or indirectly/. Moreover, <since> 5/wetland birds tend to be poor fliers and nest at ground level/, 6/ they are easy prey for domestic cats/, <and so> 7/with every new suburb, vast numbers are killed off/.

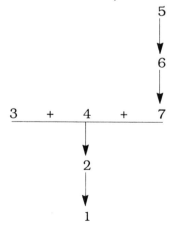

Another approach is to split up reason 2:

    2a.   Their habitat is threatened
    2b.   Their lives are threatened

The passage is then seen to contain two arguments, one for 2a and one for 2b, which converge on to 1:

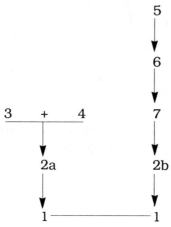

Exercise 323

1/We must stay a little longer/. 2/If we leave now we will offend your parents/, and anyway 3/the supper will be served soon/ and 4/I am starving/.

Notice how 2 does not link up with the other two reasons, and neither of them even starts to support the conclusion without the other one.

Exercise 324

1/Do not wear your high-heeled shoes to the circus, Anna/. Remember that time 2/you twisted your ankle and could not walk for three days/3/They have those same dangerous walkways at the circus/. And 4/if you snap off a heel you will have nothing to wear on Saturday night/<Anyway> 5/it would look ridiculous/ - 6/everyone else will be dressed casually/.

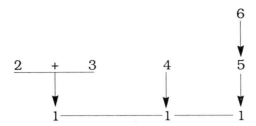

You may prefer to rewrite 2, but by cheating slightly on the marking I have got it clear enough. Remember that you are to set out the structure of the reasoning in the passage, so even if you do not think it looks ridiculous to be dressed differently, that is what it says here, so you have to depict 6 as a reason for 5.

Exercise 325

> 1/There is little point in saving money anymore/. 2/If you are trying to survive on an ordinary salary/ - and 3/few of us have any other resources/ - 2[contd]/by the time you have paid your rent and bills there is very little left/, <so that> 4/it would take you years and years to save up even for a car, let alone a house/. And 5/with inflation, by that time what you have saved will be worth next to nothing/.

There is no really satisfactory way of marking a passage like this, because it has one reason embedded in the middle of another. I have tried to show this with "2[contd]/", indicating when the interruption is over.

Another difficulty is that 3 really needs to be rewritten. Its function is to *assert* the *antecedent* of the conditional it interrupts. It can be written:

> 3. You *are* trying to survive on an ordinary salary.

Or, perhaps, that this is highly likely.

So, 2 and 3 between them entail the consequent of the conditional:

> 2a. By the time you have paid your rent and bills there is very little left.

I have included this separately on my diagram, to make the structure clearer.

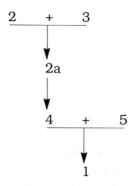

This method of *rewriting the reasons and/or conclusions* is one that we will be using frequently. If you are in doubt as to how to diagram an argument, try this:

> 1. Ask just what is being inferred from what.
> 2. Write that down in your own words, numbering reasons and conclusions.
> 3. Construct a structure diagram.

Of course you must go back and check that what you have done is a fair representation of the original.

Exercise 326

I have never been able to understand why anyone buys a brand-new car. As I figure it out, 1/they just are not worth the extra cost/. 2/A two-year-old car costs on the average no more than half the price of a new model/. And 3/major trouble is most unlikely in the first five years/. <That means> 4/you should get three good years' running for half the price of five/. And there is this: 5/about one car in twenty gives a lot of trouble right from the start/. 6/By the time it is two years old all that should have been sorted out for you/.

Unstated conclusion 7: Nobody should buy a brand-new car.

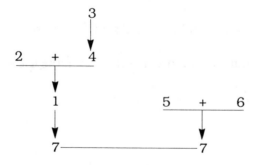

I think that it is better to read the passage as arguing for this unstated conclusion than as arguing for the statement that the author has never been able to understand why anyone buys a new car. But only a little better. Remember, we can be entirely sure of our diagrams only when the passage is entirely unambiguous, so if your diagram is not the same as mine that does *not* mean it is wrong. (Indeed, by this stage yours should be starting to be better than mine!) You should feel free to blame the author of the passage if the structure is not clear.

Exercise 327

1/Anna [has] a very strong reason for throwing in her job/. 2/At her age you do not give up a good career in head office and vanish to some tiny country town/. And 3/nothing we can say will persuade her to come back/, <which suggests that> 4/somebody or something at head office was making her life intolerable/.

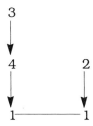

The word "must" is an inference word, not part of the statement that Anna has a strong reasons for throwing in her job.

I decided on the convergent form by asking whether 4 and 2 were being given as *independent* reasons for 1, or whether they were meant to reinforce one another. The answer seems to be that they are working independently. If you think they are reinforcing each other you should say so, and produce this diagram:

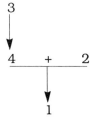

Exercise 328

Look, Tony, 1/if you plant a tree so close to the house there will be all sorts of trouble in the next few years/. 2/The main drains are just a few metres away/ and <so> 3/the roots will get in and block them/. 4/ That is very expensive to get fixed/. Then you have to think about the leaves: 5/if it is an evergreen it will shade the living room in winter/ and 6/that will not be very popular with Susan/, and 7/if it is deciduous the fallen leaves will block the gutters and mess up the yard/.

Unstated conclusion 8: Do not plant a tree so close to the house.

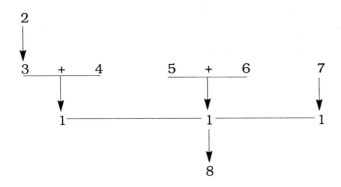

Again, although the diagram is complex it is not too hard to construct, if you start with the main conclusion and work backwards.

You may find it helps to draw several small diagrams and then bring them together at the end. That is what I often do.

Exercise 329

Statistical studies establish beyond doubt that 1/drink is to blame for most of our serious road accidents/. 2/We must make sure that nobody who has been drinking gets behind the wheel of a car/. 3/Our medical system cannot cope with the flood of accident cases/ - 2/ drunken driving must be stamped out/.

Although the diagram is simple enough, the passage does have some complexities. One is a complete lack of inference words, which makes us think hard about what is being inferred from what. Another is the repetition of the conclusion, which is why I have used "2" for two different sentences - they express much the same statement.

But the important complication is the reference to statistical studies. *This should not be included in the reasons.* As I read the passage, what is argued is that we should stamp out drunken driving because it is to blame for the road accidents, not because it has been *shown* to be to blame. These are quite different arguments. Of course you can opt for a rather more complex structure:

    1a. Statistical studies establish that drink is to blame for most of our serious road accidents.

    1b. Drink is to blame for most of our serious road accidents.

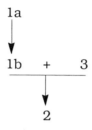

1a does entail 1b: this is built into the meaning of the term "establish".

Exercise 330

1/Mother is upset/, Harry - 2/you have made another of those ugly water stains on the table/. How many times do I have to tell you to 3/use a saucer when you have a cup of coffee/? 4/It is very expensive getting the furniture repolished/ and 5/we just cannot afford to do it again/. 6/It looks terrible too/ - imagine 7/what people must think when they see ugly stains everywhere/. And 8/what an awful example you are setting to your little sister/! I think that upsets Mother as much as the damage done to the furniture.

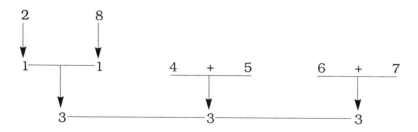

Strictly, 7 should be reworded: People will think ... when they see the stains.

Exercise 331

> 1/The engine is starting to give off a lot of smoke/, <and so> 2/it cannot be going to last much longer/. <This means> 3/we are not going to make it back home in the car/. What is more, 4/the leak in the radiator is getting worse/, <so> 5/the engine will overheat badly, especially on hills/, and remember 6/it is uphill most of the way home/. <So> again, 3/the car is not going to get us back/. <Clearly then>, 7/if we want to get home at all we will have to leave the car behind and go by bus/<so> 8/we should book our seats right now/.

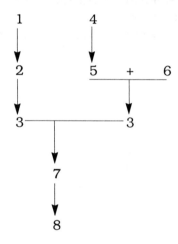

Notice how number 3 occurs *twice* in the passage. If you find a statement repeated, like this, it is important *not* to give the two occurrences different numbers. They are *not* different reasons and it a mistake to mark them differently.

Again we are reminded of the need for *very careful reading*. Marking a text is no simple mechanical process; you must attend closely to the *meaning* of every sentence. Otherwise you will miss repetitions such as the one in this passage.

Exercise 332

> 1/It is an absolute disgrace the way grown men are appearing in public in short trousers/. 2/There should be a law banning them anywhere except the beach/. Why should we have to look at ugly hairy knees in the streets and the shops? 3/It is an aesthetic assault/, and 4/we are entitled to protection/.Think of 5/the example they set to the young/! No wonder 6/they take drugs and dye their hair/ if 5/their

elders and betters do not bother to dress properly/! If these men want to complain that long trousers are uncomfortably hot, all I can say is that 7/they were good enough for better men than they/ - 8/a little discomfort is good for the character/!

Rewriting 5: Grownup men wearing shorts set a bad example to the young.

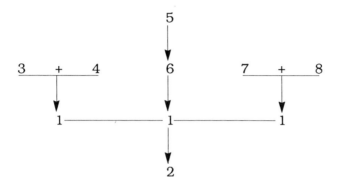

All sorts of diagram are acceptable here, as there are lots of ways of interpreting the passage. As you see, I simplify matters by ignoring some phrases, and this exercise and model answer are here largely to show you some of the shortcuts. You may not agree with what I have done to the passage, but the techniques may well come in handy in the future.

Exercise 333

1/If you buy an ice cream then Jenny will want to have one too/, and you know 2/she is not allowed to eat anything with sugar in it/ - 3/ the doctor says she has diabetes/. The trouble is 4/she does not realise how serious it is/ and 5/there will be a terrible fuss if she sees you with something she is not allowed to have/.

Unstated conclusion 6: Do not buy an ice cream.

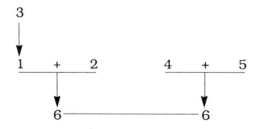

You may wonder why I include "the doctor says" in one reason but exclude "you know" from another. It looks more consistent to include both of them - or neither. Well the answer is that each case has to be treated on its own merits. In the latter case, it is the fact that she is not allowed sugar that matters, not anyone's knowledge of that fact. (When I say this matters, I mean it matters in the argument in the passage.) And in the other case, it is not because she *has* diabetes - the passage does not indeed even say that she does have diabetes - that she is not allowed sugar; it is because the doctor says so, rightly or wrongly.

Exercise 334

1/You really should turn off that radio, Tom/. You must know that 2/ it annoys the old lady next door/. 3/She needs to rest in the afternoon/ and 4/if she cannot get to sleep it upsets her digestion for days/. Anyway 5/you should be working not listening to the radio/. 6/Your exams start in three days/ and you know 7/you have hardly done any work since the summer/.

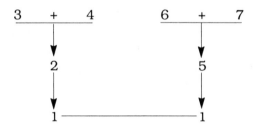

It is all right to mark "you must know that" as an inference phrase, and by now you might be used to meeting "anyway" in convergent arguments, to introduce an independent line of reasoning.

Exercise 335

1/When you get back from your trip to Korea I want you to give an illustrated talk to the Travel Club/. 2/They have never had anything about Korea/. So what say you 3/use transparency film rather than colour print film in your camera/? <That way> 4/you can put together a show where everyone can see what you are talking about/. And 5/ if they are any good you should be able to sell them to an agent or publisher/ - 6/they much prefer transparencies/ <as> 7/they give much better quality reproductions/.

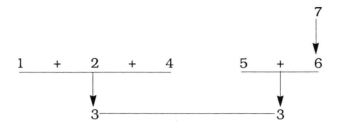

If you gave 2 as a reason for 1, that is fair enough. The way the passage is worded it could be meant to go either way, but it seemed to me to be such a *bad* reason that I read the passage the other way.

The reason I have linked 4 with 1 and 2 is that together these give a reason for taking transparencies, but separately they do not. Of course they are quite independent of 5 and 6.

Exercise 336

> 1/You must be tired/, <what with> 2/the party last night/ and 3/all that work in the garden today/. Why not 4/go to bed early/? 5/You need to be up at the crack of dawn tomorrow/. Remember 6/your flight to Sydney leaves at nine in the morning/ and 7/you want to be in good shape when you get there/, or 8/you will have no chance of getting the job/.

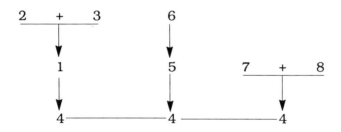

Much of this passage should be rewritten - the reasons I have marked are often not complete statements in the passage. I think that it should be obvious, in detail, just how I think that they should be rewritten, from the way I have constructed my diagram.

Exercise 337

1/All civilised countries have banned corporal punishment in schools/ 2/It is high time we followed suit/. 3/The practice is thoroughly discredited/ as damaging for students and teachers alike: 4/bad for teachers/ <because> 5/it encourages them to become tyrannical and sadistic/and 6/a good teacher must be exactly the opposite/; 7/bad for the pupils/ <because> 8/it is degrading. Unless they are treated like adults rather than performing animals/ 9/they will never learn to conduct themselves with maturity and dignity/. The other problem with corporal punishment is that 10/it does not work/. <Indeed>, 11/ the worst trouble-makers amongst the pupils take advantage of it as a means of drawing further attention to themselves/.

Rewriting some of the statements:

3. Corporal punishment is thoroughly discredited.
4. Corporal punishment is bad for teachers.
7. Corporal punishment is bad for pupils.
8. With corporal punishment pupils are treated like performing animals rather than adults.
9. If pupils are not treated like adults they will never learn to conduct themselves with maturity and dignity.

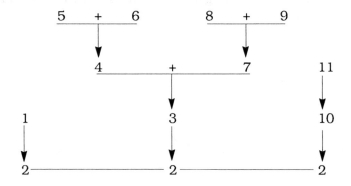

In this exercise we have almost reached the stage where marking the reasons and conclusions directly on the text is a waste of time. When it becomes too difficult, the thing to do is give up, and, *instead,* write out *all* of the reasons and conclusions in your own words. Of course you run the risk of departing from the argument in the passage, but remember that it is precisely because the argument in the passage is difficult to portray, as written, that you are taking this step of rewording it.

So feel free to express the reasons and conclusions in your own words. This is especially useful with very long passages of text. Indeed, sometimes the pattern of reasoning in a whole book can be represented in a dozen or so reasons and conclusions and displayed in a diagram. In this case you will almost certainly have to use your own words.

Exercise 338

I vote 1/we eat out tonight/. 2/There is nothing in the fridge/ <so> 3/if we are going to cook our own we will have to go shopping/, and 4/the car is not going/ <so> 5/that would mean carrying it all back home/ and 6/I am far too tired for that/. And listen, 7/there is this new fish restaurant they are all talking about/. 8/Jan went there last week and had a whole fish done that spicy Szechwan way/ - 9/your favourite/.

Rewriting:

1. Let us eat out tonight.
8. The new restaurant serves spicy Szechwan whole fish.
9. That is your favourite.

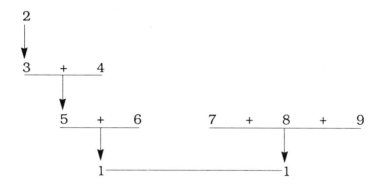

Exercise 339

1/We really should help Aunt Jean tidy up her garden this weekend/ 2/It has become such a mess that the neighbours are complaining it spoils the street/, and 3/we do not want to upset that Mr Jones over the road/ - <after all> 4/he is our bank manager/. And remember, 5/ she is fairly well off/.Who knows, 6/she may leave some of it to us/, <and then> 7/we will be able to pay off the mortgage/ <and so> 8/you can get that new car/. Anyway, even if she gives it all to a cats' home, 1/we still should give her a hand/ - <after all> 9/she is your poor mother's only sister/.

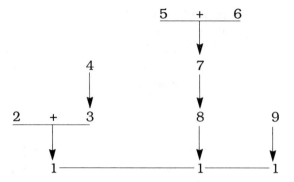

We might well add an intermediate conclusion, that it is to our advantage to help her. This would link 2 + 3 with 8, feeding into 1, and would highlight the (ethically) important difference between all of those considerations and the last one, 9. Then the diagram would look like this:

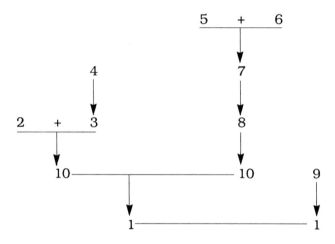

Unstated intermediate conclusion 10: It is to our advantage to help her.

Exercise 340

1/David is simply hopeless at playing the violin/ - 2/his wrist is not supple enough/ and 3/his fingers are too short/, <so> 4/he cannot reach the strings properly/, and anyway 5/his ear is not anywhere near good enough to play it in tune/. <So> 6/<u>he should give up the violin and switch to the flute</u>/. 7/That would be easier to live with/. 8/Nobody can make a really horrible noise on a flute, not even David/ And 9/we would not have to buy him a new instrument/. Remember that 10/his violin is in very poor condition/, but 11/he could use Mary's flute/ 12/which is as good as new/.

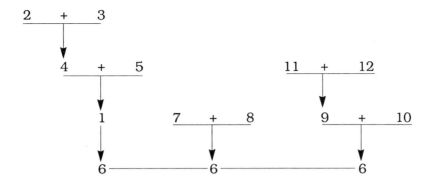

Another approach would be to divide this into two separate and distinct arguments, one for the conclusion that he should give up the violin and the other for the conclusion that he should take up the flute.

Valid
Inferences   4

This chapter presents an ideal model of argumentation, in which, if the reasons are true, the truth of the conclusion is thereby guaranteed. Such arguments are described as *valid*.

Of course in practice we often have to make do with less reliable arguments, but it is important to have a clear idea of how a valid argument works, and how to test for validity.

Validity defined

> An argument is valid when and only when the truth of the reasons would guarantee the truth of the conclusion.

Note that the reasons do not have to be true. The requirement is that if they were true then they would guarantee that the conclusion is true as well. Thus for example:

> Sydney is in Hungary and Hungary is in South America, so Sydney is in South America.

The reasons are both false: Sydney is in Australia not Hungary, and Hungary is in Europe not South America, but if these two reasons *were* true then the conclusion would have to be true as well. There is no way that Sydney could be in Hungary and Hungary in South America without Sydney being in South America.

A test of validity

Here is a useful test of validity:

> Assuming the reasons to be true,
> is it possible for the conclusion to be false?
> If this is possible the inference is invalid.

In practice it is usually safe to assume that the opposite holds too: if this is impossible the inference is valid. There are some exceptions, though, so if you have any doubts you should apply the definition as well - make sure that the reasons, if true, would *guarantee* the truth of the conclusion. That test *always* works.

Form and validity

Consider the Sydney argument. We could make all manner of *substitutions* and still have a valid argument. Replace "Sydney" with "London", "Hungary" with "Thailand", and "South America" with "the Antarctic" and we get this:

London is in Thailand and Thailand is in the Antarctic, so London is in the Antarctic.

This is valid too, and for the same reason as the original. All of these argument share a common *form*. They are all instances of this schema:

A is in B and B is in C, so A is in C.

And any argument of this form is valid (provided "in" is used in the same sense as in the Sydney example).

We say that an argument form is valid if *every* argument which is an instance of that form is valid. An argument form is fallacious if there are some instances of the form which are invalid.

To show that a form is valid it is not enough to find some valid instances. A fallacious form can have any number of valid instances. A single invalid instance makes an argument form fallacious. To be a valid argument form, *all* of the instances must be valid.

There are many valid argument forms. Formal logicians study these in detail, trying to give systematic accounts of why certain forms are valid while others are not. Although it would be a diversion for us to go at all deeply into this, there are a few standard forms which can teach us something about the nature of valid inference.

Valid and fallacious forms

Consider four inferences, all with one reason in common but differing in their other reasons and in their conclusions:

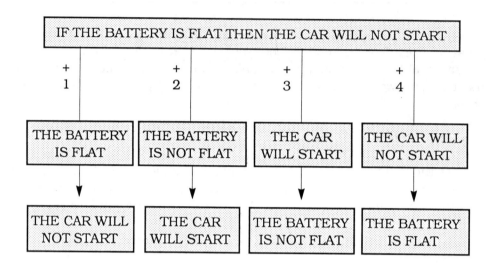

Four separate arguments are represented. They all share the reason: "If the battery is flat then the car will not start." The four conclusions are at the bottom of the diagram.

The shared reason is a *conditional* statement. It has two ingredients: the *antecedent* statement, that the battery is flat, and the *consequent* statement, that the car will not start. Neither the antecedent nor the consequent is affirmed when a conditional statement is made. It is not affirmed that the battery is flat, and neither is it affirmed that the car will not start. All that is affirmed is that *if* the battery is flat *then* the car will not start. In particular, nothing is said about whether the car will start if the battery is not flat.

Which (if any) of the four inferences are valid? In which cases would the truth of the reasons guarantee the truth of the conclusion?

1. If the battery is flat then the car will not start, and the battery is flat, therefore the car will not start.

If both of these reasons are true, then the truth of the conclusion is guaranteed. This inference is valid.

2. If the battery is flat then the car will not start, but the battery is not flat, therefore the car will start.

Here the conclusion does not follow. There could be something *else* wrong with the car, say a broken distributor, so that it still will not start but for a completely different reason. Thus the truth of the reasons does not guarantee the truth of the conclusion.

3. If the battery is flat then the car will not start, but the car will start, therefore the battery is not flat.

As in the first case, if both of these reasons are true then the conclusion has to be true as well.

4. If the battery is flat then the car will not start, and the car will not start, therefore the battery is flat.

This conclusion does not follow. Suppose that the reasons are both true but that the battery is not flat - again the distributor is broken. In these circumstances the reasons are true but the conclusion is false. Nothing about why the car will not start follows from these reasons.

These forms of valid and fallacious argument can be represented symbolically, and have technical names:

VALID FORMS	FALLACIES
1 Modus Ponens	2 Denying the Antecedent
If P then Q P Therefore Q	If P then Q Not-P Therefore not-Q
3 Modus Tollens	4 Affirming the Consequent
If P then Q Not-Q Therefore not-P	If P then Q Q Therefore P

Although we have been working with specific examples, these results are general. Any argument of form 1 or 3 will be valid; Any argument of form 2 or 4 is suspect.

Technical terms and Ps and Qs

We are using quite a few technical terms here. You may be relieved to learn that there is no real need to remember them. We will be developing techniques which will enable you to work directly on the examples you meet without trying to fit them into formal categories. The only reason that the technical terms are being used here is that these "standard" forms illustrate clearly how an argument can be valid.

Also, if you are not used to working with Ps and Qs, do not worry. There will not be much of it, and it can usually be eliminated.

A final point. It does not matter what letters are used in these formulae. For example,

If P then Q	If Q then P
P	Q
Therefore Q	Therefore P

are alternative ways of presenting Modus Ponens, and you can use A and B or X and Y or whatever you like instead of P and Q.

Another valid form: Disjunctive Syllogism

If we know that one or the other of two statements is true, and then find out that one of them is false, we can validly infer that the other one is true.

> Either John is in the bathroom or the door is jammed.
> John is not in the bathroom.
> Therefore the door is jammed.

If both reasons are true then the truth of the conclusion is guaranteed. There is no way that these reasons could be true and the conclusion false.

This is another of the standard valid forms:

> Either P or Q
> Not-P
> Therefore Q

This time the order of P and Q does not matter, in the first reason.

Valid inference in practice

Inferences that follow these standard forms - both the valid forms and the fallacious ones - are not uncommon. But there are lots and lots of inferences that do not fit these patterns, indeed that do not conform to any such system. The reason for discussing a few of them was not to provide a practical way of finding out whether an inference is valid. Rather, it was to illustrate with simple and rather idealised examples just how it is that truth is preserved in a valid inference, but need not be in an invalid one.

When you are confronted with real-life examples of inference, usually it is best to work straight from the general test of validity:

> Assuming the reasons to be true, is it possible for the conclusion to be false?

One of the main aims of this book is to give you an opportunity to apply this test to a wide range of examples. But a preliminary move will help. One of the difficulties many people encounter is with conclusions they know very well are true. Suppose we have an inference whose conclusion is that there are six states in Australia - this is true, and so how can we ask about circumstances in which it is false?

To help with this it is a good idea to think about the difference between statements which *are* true but *could* be false, and statements which are true but could *not* be false.

1. There are six states in Australia.
2. Six is divisible by three.

It is not difficult to conceive of circumstances in which 1 would turn out to be false - if for example the Northern Territory became a state, or Queensland broke away from Australia. In the first case there would be seven states, and in the second only five, providing everything else stays the same. These are *possibilities.* But it is not easy to think of any circumstances in which 2 would turn out to be false. Indeed, it is impossible. There are no such circumstances. Not only is 2 true - it is *necessarily* true.

(I do not want to make my explanation hinge on any particular example, so if you have any doubts about 2, any of these might serve as well:

3. Mothers are older than their daughters.
4. Every effect has a cause.
5. Uncles are male.

Note that in 4 the word is "effect", not "event".)

Exercises

Turn to Exercise Four and work on numbers 401-412.

Pairs of statements

The next step is to consider *pairs* of statements. Remember the test for a valid inference - the conclusion cannot be false when the reasons are true. To decide whether this is the case you have to think of two statements *together*. As another preliminary, the next section of Exercise Four is designed to help you get used to handling them two at a time. You are given a pair of statements, like

A.   It is raining somewhere
B.   It is raining somewhere nearby

and are asked whether either of these can validly be inferred from the other. To decide this, try to find conditions in which A is true while B is false, and conversely, conditions in which B is true while A is false.

Thus here, A is true while B is false if for example it is raining a long way away but not nearby. But there are no possible conditions in which B is true while A is false, because anywhere nearby is *some*where. So, A can validly be inferred from B, but not B from A.

A note on terminology. When one statement can validly be inferred from another, we say that the latter *implies* or *entails* the former:

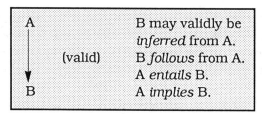

A		B may validly be inferred from A.
(valid)	B *follows* from A.
		A *entails* B.
B		A *implies* B.

Exercises

Turn to Exercise 4 and work on numbers 413-420.

The unstated reason test

You have met the accountant example more than once. In the first Chapter it went like this:

He is an accountant, so he is probably mean.

We handled it by asking what has to be *added* to the reason to make sure that the conclusion follows. Remember that we noticed two little traps, involving the words "he" and "probably", and cunningly concluded that all you *have* to add is this:

Most male accountants are mean.

Now you will see that when we *add* this as a reason we *rule out all of the ways in which the conclusion could be false,* given the truth of the reason. The argument:

He is an accountant, and most male accountants are mean, so he is probably mean

is a completely valid one. This is a powerful method.

The first step is to look at the reasons and the conclusion stated, and ask:

> What extra reasons have to be added,
> to turn this into a valid inference?

Write them down.

These are often called the *unstated reasons.*

Make sure that what you add are suitably *general* statements about classes, not particular statements about the individuals (if any) mentioned in the argument.

So, if the argument is that Paul must have grey hair because he is a professor, add the general statement that all male professors have grey hair, not the particular statement that if Paul is a professor then he has grey hair.

Also, make sure that the reason you add is as *weak* as possible. In doing this, include any relevant restrictions which are mentioned in the argument or which are clearly implicit.

Thus in the accountant example, the added reason is explicitly about *male* accountants and makes only the weak claim that *most* of them are mean, rather than the stronger claim that *all* of them are. Likewise, "Paul" is a name used usually for males.

(A note on terminology. What I call "unstated reasons" or "added reasons" are called all sorts of things in other books: missing or suppressed or unstated reasons or premises or assumptions - almost all combinations are used.)

In the midst of all this detail do not lose sight of the most important point: if *anything* which could possibly be false needs to be added to the reasons to make sure that the conclusion follows, then the inference as stated is *not valid*.

Exercises

Turn to Exercise 4 and work on numbers 421-440.

False statements

An argument can be *valid* and have any or all of its reasons and conclusions *false.* To give a trivial example:

> The planet Earth has no moons.
> Planets that have no moons have no gravity.
> Therefore the planet Earth has no gravity.

We all know that the first reason is false, and that the conclusion is false. And the scientists insist that every object exerts gravitational forces on other objects, so even if there are planets without moons, they will have gravity. Thus, the second reason is also false.

But if we *assume* that these two reasons are true, then the conclusion must also be true. There is no way in which these reasons can be true and the conclusion false. That is, the inference is *valid.*

One problem is that many of us find it very hard to ignore the question of whether the statements are true or false. It is easy to get sidetracked into finding out just which planets do have moons and what the scientists *do* say about moons and gravity. Because many find this difficult, Exercises 441-450 are simple exercises designed to help you to work confidently with false statements.

EXERCISE FOUR

For questions one to twelve, describe circumstances in which the statement would be false. In each case, try to think of at least three independent sets of circumstances.
Note that you may not be able to give circumstances in which the statement

is *definitely* false. In the Australia example, if Queensland breaks away that does not *in itself* ensure that there are not six states - New Zealand may join up simultaneously. All that you need to describe are circumstances in which, other things being equal, the statement would turn out to be false.

401   It often rains in London.

402   Shoes come in pairs - one left one right.

403   There are 26 letters in the English alphabet.

404   Purcell is not very well known.

405   Europeans have pale skins.

406   They ski a lot in Austria.

407   In 1987, Reagan was president of the USA.

408   Shirts that have sleeves have two of them.

409   Beethoven is a great composer.

410   Iron is used for the core of electro-magnets.

411   Aspirin is commonly used to cure headaches.

412   In Fiji they drink a lot of kava.

In each of these next questions there is a pair of statements. Can either of them be inferred validly from the other one? Which, from which? Explain why. If the statements are vague or ambiguous, consider whether this bears on the question of what follows from what?

413 a. You own a motorcar.
      b. You own a vehicle.

414 a. It is raining where you are right now as you read this.
      b. It is raining half a mile away from where you are right now.

415 a. You are reading.
      b. You are reading a newspaper.

416 a. The sky is purple.
     b. The sky is coloured.

417 a. You are thirty feet tall.
     b. You are taller than any elephant.

418 a. Starlings eat vast quantities of grain.
     b. Starlings cost the farmers a small fortune.

419 a. $2 + 2 = 4$.
     b. $2 + 2 = 5$.

420 a. Foreigners are bringing AIDS into Samoa.
     b. Foreigners should be tested for AIDS before entering Samoa.

In Questions 421-430 you are given two statements which are numbered 1 and 3. Write down another statement, 2, such that the inference from 1 + 2 to 3 is valid.

Explain your choice.

421 1. The cinema is right in the centre of town.
     3. You do not have a chance of finding a carpark anywhere near to it.

422 1. Last year Mary failed half of her courses and barely passed the others.
     3. She would be wise to study Geography rather than Philosophy this year.

423 1. That car is only two years old.
     3. I will not be able to afford it.

424 1. You will need to refer to this book almost daily for years.
     3. You should buy a hardback copy.

425 1. There are heavy dark clouds forming over the mountains.
     3. It is going to rain very soon.

426 1. Bach was employed as an organist and choirmaster.
     3. He wrote a lot of church music.

427 1. The Americans can afford to spend huge sums on research and development.
     3. It will be impossible for any other country to win the America's Cup.

428 1. Tom rides a motorbike.
3. He will have an accident before the year is over.

429 1. There are bacon bones in the soup.
3. Anna will not eat it.

430 1. This insecticide has been passed for general use by the Department of Agriculture.
3. It is perfectly safe for me to use it.

In Exercises 431-440, what reason(s) must be added to yield a valid inference? Explain where necessary.

If any of the statements are vague or ambiguous, clarify them.

431 The roof of the water tank must reflect as much heat as possible. Bitumen is therefore quite unsuitable, being such a dark colour.

432 I have added some blue paint to the red paint in this can, so now the paint in the can will be purple.

433 According to United Nations experts, close to two in every three people in the world today are likely to be denied some basic human rights. This means that the governments of most countries are repressive.

434 Charles will have to sit in the enclosure. Only Members are allowed in the Grandstand.

435 The misfortunes of others inevitably make us reflect on how fortunate we are, and that keeps us humble. So it is after all a good thing that others suffer their misfortunes.

436 Choral music differs from instrumental music because of the limited range and endurance of the human voice.

437 The Volkswagen Beetle is quite unlike any other car because of its aircooled engine and amazing reliability.

438 I'm feeling hungry and there's nothing in the fridge, so let's go downtown.

439 I must take regular exercise - I need to get fit again.

440 When the first men landed on the moon everybody was thrilled because it showed that space travel is really possible after all.

441 Here is a *false statement:*

London is the capital of France.

Many people find it difficult even to write false statements. So here is a chance for some practice. Simply write down some false statements, like the one about London. Write down nine of them.

442 I hope that number 441 was easy. Did you manage to cover a good range of topics? If not, go back and change some of them. Then, write down a false statement that follows validly from each of the false statements you wrote down in 441. (So in the case of "London is the capital of France," I could write down "London is not in England.")

443 to 450: Using only reasons which you are fairly sure are false, construct an entertaining and valid argument in support of each of these conclusions. Try to vary your patterns of argumentation. Explain if necessary.

443 Ice cream contains a lot of vitamins.

444 There are no plants in the Antarctic.

445 Rich people are always happier than poor ones.

446 Eating raw carrots gives you amazingly good eyesight.

447 Children usually know what is best for them.

448 If you watch a lot of television you will forget how to read.

449 It is easy to learn how to play a musical instrument if you are good at mathematics.

450 Lightning never strikes the same place twice.

EXERCISE FOUR - MODEL ANSWERS

Exercise 401

It often rains in London

False if;
1. An ice age freezes all the seas so that it never rains any more.
2. A huge dome is built to turn London into an entirely underground city.
3. A nuclear war reverses the prevailing winds so that England usually receives dry air from continental Europe.

Exercise 402

Shoes come in pairs - one left one right.

False if;
1. Most people have three feet.
2. Most people have only one foot.
3. Left and right feet are the same shape, and people prefer to get one spare when they are buying shoes.

Exercise 403

There are 26 letters in the English alphabet

False if;
1. The letter "q" is dropped, being replaced with "kw".
2. The letter "c" is dropped, being replaced with "k" or "s" as appropriate.
3. Separate letters are introduced for long and short vowels.

Exercise 404

Purcell is not very well known.

False if;
1. He lives long enough to write a lot more music.
2. They play much more of his music on the radio.
3. Young people suddenly "discover" him.

Exercise 405

Europeans have pale skins.

False if;
1. Europeans all mate with dark-skinned people and have dark offspring.
2. The earth's climate changes so that Europeans' skin becomes dark.
3. A skin-darkening drug becomes so fashionable that nobody is left with a pale skin.

Note that as stated none of these make it false now that Europeans have pale skins. If that worries you, make 1 to 3 all refer to some time in the past such that, had these conditions then obtained, it would now be false that Europeans have pale skins.

Exercise 406

They ski a lot in Austria.

False if;
1. The climate changes so that there is no snow any more in Austria.
2. The Austrian government bans skiing.
3. A nuclear accident contaminates Austria and everyone leaves, even the skiers.

Exercise 407

In 1987, Reagan was president of the USA.

False if;
1. He resigns because of ill health in 1986.
2. He loses a presidential election in 1984.
3. World War III wipes out the USA in 1985.

Exercise 408

Shirts that have sleeves have two of them.

False if;
1. People have four arms.
2. People prefer to keep the left arm inside the shirt all the time.
3. People like to have a spare sleeve, in the back of the shirt, just in case.

Exercise 409

Beethoven is a great composer.

False if;
1. He turns deaf so early that he loses interest.
2. As a young man he studies philosophy and thereafter never has time for anything else.
3. He dies at the age of eighteen months.

Exercise 410

Iron is used for the core of electro-magnets.

False if;
1. Iron is far too rare and expensive for that.
2. Iron is not strongly magnetic.
3. Iron corrodes too quickly.

Exercise 411

Aspirin is commonly used to cure headaches.

False if;
1. People develop an immunity to the effects of aspirin.
2. Aspirin proves to have a disastrous long-term genetic effect and is banned.
3. A more effective and safer cheap alternative drug is available, and replaces aspirin.

Exercise 412

In Fiji they drink a lot of kava.

False if;
1. Drinking kava is effectively banned in Fiji.
2. The people there take a sudden dislike to it.
3. A virus wipes out the tree whose root is used for making kava.

Exercise 413

a. You own a motorcar
b. You own a vehicle

The inference from a to b is valid, but not the inference from b to a. A motor car is a vehicle, so it can never be true that you own a motorcar but false that you own a vehicle. On the other hand, if you own a motorcycle but no motorcar then it is true that you own a vehicle but false that you own a motorcar.

Exercise 414

    a. It is raining where you are right now as you read this
    b. It is raining half a mile away from where you are right now

a is true and b is false if you are in a patch of rain only a hundred yards wide, and there is no other rain anywhere nearby.

b is true and a is false if the only patch of rain for miles is half a mile away and is only a hundred yards wide.

Exercise 415

    a. You are reading
    b. You are reading a newspaper

a is true and b is false when you are reading this. So b cannot validly be inferred from a. On the other hand, there are no conditions under which b is true while a is false - a can validly be inferred from b. If you are reading a newspaper then you must be reading.

Exercise 416

    a. The sky is purple
    b. The sky is coloured

a is true and b is false - never: because purple is a colour.
b is true and a is false when the sky is green (all over).

Exercise 417

    a. You are thirty feet tall
    b. You are taller than any elephant

Although if you are indeed thirty feet tall you will in fact be taller than any elephant, a does not entail b. To infer b validly from a one needs the extra statement that no elephants *are* thirty feet tall. This is true, but it has to be stated. And of course b does not entail a either. If the tallest elephant is sixteen feet tall and you are seventeen, you are well short of thirty feet tall.

Exercise 418

    a. Starlings eat vast quantities of grain
    b. Starlings cost the farmers a small fortune

a is true and b is false if starlings eat only grain that is left behind after harvest.

b is true and a is false if starlings are carnivores but their droppings frequently ruin expensive farm machinery.

Exercise 419

    a. $2 + 2 = 4$
    b. $2 + 2 = 5$

Applying the usual test for validity: a is true and b is false - always. Under all conditions a is true; under all conditions b is false. b is true and a is false - never. There are and can be no conditions under which b is true, or under which a is false.

If we are not careful we might infer that a can validly be inferred from b. That is, the statement that $2 + 2 = 4$ follows from the statement that $2 + 2 = 5$. And that is ridiculous: How could the truth of $2 + 2 = 4$ be guaranteed by the truth of $2 + 2 = 5$?

This is one of the exceptions mentioned early in the chapter, where the definition of validity has to be used, not just the test for invalidity.

Exercise 420

    a. Foreigners are bringing AIDS into Samoa
    b. Foreigners should be tested for AIDS before entering Samoa

a is true and b is false if there is no test for AIDS.
b is true and a is false if AIDS has not yet arrived in Samoa but is likely to do so.

Note: Often in the following exercises there will be all sorts of alternatives to the unstated reasons written down in these answers.

Exercise 421

Reason 1: The cinema is right in the centre of town.

Conclusion 3: You do not have a chance of finding a carpark anywhere near to it.

Unstated reason 2: You do not have a chance of finding a carpark anywhere near the centre of town.

Exercise 422

Reason 1: Last year Mary failed half of her courses and barely passed the others.

Conclusion 3: She would be wise to study Geography rather than Philosophy this year.

Unstated reason 2a: People who do as badly as that may pass Geography but will not pass Philosophy.

Unstated reason 2b: Philosophy is harder than Geography.

When you think about it, even 2a is not enough to make sure of the conclusion. We need also the statement that she has to study one or the other. Without that, she may be wiser to do something altogether different.

Some people hold to the view that philosophy is more or less impossible, in which case the truth of 2b is more or less assured, independently.

Joking aside, it is fairly clear that the sort of reason we want for 2b is something like what I have written down - some more general consideration than in 2a. But when you think about it, it could be that Mary is one of those odd ones who do really well at Philosophy and poorly at everything else, that she did only "safe" subjects last year, and that if she changes to Philosophy she will do really well for once.

And in this perfectly comprehensible if uncommon sort of case both 2a and 2b are false, for different reasons. In the case of 2a it is simply false that all people like that will not pass Philosophy - Mary is fairly sure to. And 2b may be true for most people but not for Mary.

Perhaps then the trouble is simply that I made a very bad initial choice for 2a and 2b? What do you think?

Exercise 423

Reason 1: That car is only two years old.

Conclusion 3: I will not be able to afford it.

Unstated reason 2: I cannot afford any car that is only two years old.

I was about to type "that is two *or less* years old", in 2, and then realised that

I was assuming that cars get cheaper as they get older. A safe enough assumption perhaps, but still it is an assumption. Hence my more cautious wording.

Note that "I cannot afford any car at all" does the job for 2 but it does it too well: it is stronger than is needed, and so makes the inference look worse than it is.

Exercise 424

Reason 1: You will need to refer to this book almost daily for years.

Conclusion 3: You should buy a hardback copy.

Unstated reason 2a: You will need to buy a copy and only a hardback copy will stand up to such heavy use.

Unstated reason 2b: You will need to have a copy and a paperback will probably wear out.

Notice that 2a refers to buying a copy and 2b to having one. As students quickly discover, this is an important difference.

There is another respect in which 2b is weaker than 2a. It is a matter of fact not logic that there are only two versions of a typical book - hardback and paperback. There is also the logical possibility of some other version that will (probably) not wear out and which is neither a paperback nor a hardback. Reason 2b leaves this possibility open.

Exercise 425

Reason 1: There are heavy dark clouds forming over the mountains.

Conclusion 3: It is going to rain very soon.

Unstated reason 2: When heavy dark clouds form over the mountains here it is sure to rain very soon.

Notice that I have made the claim a *local* one. Rather than invoke some universal law of nature about mountains and clouds and rain, all we need is an item of local knowledge - that when there are heavy clouds over *these* mountains it will rain.

I cannot give you any *rule* for deciding how general the unstated reasons should be, other than this: Make them as general as you reasonably can.

Exercise 426

Reason 1: Bach was employed as an organist and choirmaster.

Conclusion 3: He wrote a lot of church music.

Unstated reason 2a: Organists and choirmasters have to write a lot of church music. (Warning - read on.)

Unstated reason 2b: Most organists and choirmasters write a lot of church music. (Warning - read on.)

The inference here from 1 to 3 is a particularly bad one. Perhaps if we take it as explaining why he wrote so much of that *sort* of music it is fair, but I am told that nowadays at least your average choirmaster/organist never has to write a note.

The weakness of the inference is exactly paralleled in the inaccuracy of 2a - the reason needed to get from 1 to 3. And 2b is not much closer to the truth.

But wait. In 2a we could have referred specifically to Bach's time and place. Consider:

2aa.   When Bach was active organists and choirmasters in Ger many had to write a lot of church music.

This could well be true when 2a is well wide of the mark.

Again we see how a slight change of wording can make a great difference. Which should we choose? I think I prefer 2aa to 2a, and would replace 2b with

2ba.   When Bach was active most organists and choirmasters in Germany had to write a lot of church music.

I hope that by now you are thoroughly weaned from the habit of asking at an early stage whether any of these statements are actually true. Eventually we will want to know, but as I have said so often, at this stage that is not our concern, and it is surprising how far we can get without worrying about truth values as opposed to validity.

Exercise 427

Reason 1: The Americans can afford to spend huge sums on research and development.

Conclusion 3: It will be impossible for any other country to win the America's Cup.

Unstated reason 2: Nobody but the Americans will be able to spend huge sums, and without doing so they have no chance of winning.

I have been careful not to refer to what they can afford, for as we all should know, it is possible not to spend sums you can afford and also possible to spend sums you cannot afford. Thus the argument also has to state that the Americans will spend these huge sums, not just that they can afford them.

Exercise 428

Reason 1: Tom rides a motorbike.

Conclusion 3: He will have an accident before the year is over.

Unstated reason 2a: If you ride a motorbike you will have an accident very soon.

Unstated reason 2b: Most motorcyclists have accidents.

This feels rather artificial. 2a has been constructed "by formula", and is too far from the truth. I mean, the argument surely is not as bad as that, is it?

Try some alternatives:
    2aa.   Tom is a reckless sort of fellow and people like that are sure to have an accident if they ride a motorbike.

That sounds rather more plausible, and it does the job as well as 2a does. The reference to Tom specifically is a trifle worrying, though. How do we know to use 2aa and not this?

    2ab.   Tom is a chimpanzee and they always have accidents when they ride motorbikes.

That too, when added to 1, gives a valid inference to 3.

So you see there may be something dubious about making any specific reference to Tom at all in the unstated reason. What I mean is that perhaps we cannot say anything new about Tom specifically in the extra reason. Not that he is a chimpanzee, or that he is a reckless sort of fellow. Perhaps we must confine ourselves to extra statements about whole classes of whom Tom has already been stated to be a member -- such as motorcyclists.

While we are in these deep waters I shall take the opportunity of mentioning the cheapest trick of all. You already know one easy way to make any inference valid: Add the reason

If R then C

where R is the sum of the reasons and C the conclusion. (Do you know what is wrong with this move?) Here is another: Add the statement C to the reasons! The inference from R + C to C is always a valid one. (Can you work out what is wrong with this move too?)

Exercise 429

Reason 1: There are bacon bones in the soup.

Conclusion 3: Anna will not eat it.

Unstated reason 2: Anna will not eat anything with bacon bones.

It is tempting to make 2 stronger: Anna will not eat anything with pig-meat in it, or even anything with meat in it. But the argument does not require that. She may indeed be happy to eat meat, even from pigs, but has this particular aversion to bacon, maybe just to bacon bones, or perhaps to bones. Hence the cautious wording of 2.

Exercise 430

Reason 1: This insecticide has been passed for general use by the Department of Agriculture.

Conclusion 3: It is perfectly safe for me to use it.

Unstated reasons:
2a. Anything passed by the Department of Agriculture will be perfectly safe.

2b. The Department of Agriculture knows what is safe and what isn't.

Conditions in which 2b is true while 2a is false: The Department knows that the insecticide is unsafe but is bribed into passing it for general use. Unlikely, one hopes, but the fact that one can hope this shows that it is possible. And this one is more than a remote possibility in some places, I am told.

Exercise 431

The roof of the water tank must reflect as much heat as possible. Bitumen is therefore quite unsuitable, being such a dark colour.

Unstated reason: Dark colours reflect less heat than pale ones do.

Exercise 432

I have added some blue paint to the red paint in this can, so now the paint in the can will be purple.

Unstated reason: Red paint plus blue paint makes purple paint.

I have already commented in sufficient detail on one aspect of this, but there is another. You will notice that I did not say that the unstated reason is this:

Red plus blue equals purple.

The reason I have given has another important ingredient - paint. That is, it entails this:

Paint plus paint equals paint.

Had you noticed that the argument is assuming this too? From a logical point of view you might get wine, or elephants, or yesterday's newspaper. So I have ruled out all of those by including the statement that the result of the mixing will be paint. The argument does assume this.

Exercise 433

According to United Nations experts, close to two in every three people in the world today are likely to be denied some basic human rights. This means that the governments of most countries are repressive.

Unstated reason: Denials of basic human rights stem from governmental repression.

There is no need to refer to the numbers: two out of three is "most".

Exercise 434

Charles will have to sit in the enclosure. Only Members are allowed in the Grandstand.

Unstated reason: Charles is not a member.

This time I have not been so fussy. I hope that you have though. The argument also assumes that those who are not allowed in the Grandstand must sit in the enclosure. State that too - it does not go without saying. And note that that contains two statements: that they must sit, and that they must be in the enclosure. This is perhaps obvious, but it is worth making some fuss about, because one of the obvious counterexamples that comes to mind is where Charles elects to go home in a huff, or spends the day in the bar.

Exercise 435

> The misfortunes of others inevitably make us reflect on how fortunate we are, and that keeps us humble. So it is after all a good thing that others suffer their misfortunes.

Unstated reason: It is good to be humble, and that makes up for the suffering. As a first attempt, the first part on its own looks promising, but it is nowhere near strong enough. The argument needs the statement that the good (our humility) outweighs the bad (the suffering of others).

There is an important general point here, often overlooked. It is all very well to argue that if we perform some action there will be good consequences, but this does not even start to be an adequate argument for performing it unless we also know that there will not be too much in the way of bad consequences.

This is why the argument about misfortune sounds so callous. It is assuming not just that it is good to be humble but also that this actually makes up for the suffering. For the suffering of innocent outsiders, at that. I am prepared to grant that a tiny bit of suffering can be outweighed, but not a great deal of it. It is a bad thing if others suffer. All that the argument can hope to show is that it is not quite so bad if it happens to have some good consequence, such as making "us" humble.

Exercise 436

> Choral music differs from instrumental music because of the limited range and endurance of the human voice.

Unstated reason: A limited range and endurance is a bad thing.

Perhaps my tastes are showing here, but I am taking it that the conclusion means that choral music is not as good as instrumental. If you think it means something different then you will need a different unstated reason.

I do not think that the argument assumes that musical instruments do not have these limitations - I think that this is *said* in the passage, even if we cannot identify any particular string of words which does this. But again, if you disagree you should include this in the unstated reason. I am not going to argue this point. It is a matter of interpretation of an ambiguous passage, and that would be a waste of time.

Exercise 437

> The Volkswagen Beetle is quite unlike any other car because of its aircooled engine and amazing reliability.

Unstated reason: What? I was tempted to write: No other car is like this. But that is the conclusion!
I see two ways out. One is to interpret "The Volkswagen Beetle is quite unlike any other car" as saying that it is *better* than any other. Then the unstated reason is that aircooled engines and amazing reliability are unparalleled virtues, in a car, and that the Beetle alone exhibits them.

Another way, which is really a way of doing the same thing, is to insist that both of the statements presented in the passage are reasons, for the *unstated conclusion* that the Beetle is better than any other car.

On the other hand, perhaps we can read the passage as arguing that the Beetle is an exceptionally *bad* car, because of its (noisy) aircooled engine and (boring) reliability.

Exercise 438

> I'm feeling hungry and there's nothing in the fridge, so let's go downtown.

Unstated reason: (First time through I am leaving this blank, and here is why..)

A way of handling this is to ask, first, what *does* follow from the reasons stated. Answer: If I am going to eat I will have to look somewhere other than the fridge.

And what has to be added to that to get the conclusion? Answer: The other place to look is downtown. So now:

Unstated reason: The other place to look is downtown.

Still the conclusion does not quite follow. For example, logically speaking it does not matter who finds the food, so long as I get to eat it.

Exercise 439

I must take regular exercise - I need to get fit again.

Unstated reason: Only regular exercise will get me fit again.

That gets us at least to the conclusion that I need to take regular exercise. Does it follow that I must do this? What say this is a very minor need? Then it would be excessive to infer that I *must* do it.

For this reason I want to add another reason: My need to get fit again is a very important need. You may think that it goes without saying, but if in doubt - say it anyway.

Exercise 440

When the first men landed on the moon everybody was thrilled because it showed that space travel is really possible after all.

Not an easy one! First, do not break this up too finely:

1/When the first men landed on the moon everybody was thrilled/ <because> 2/it showed that space travel is really possible after all/.

The reason is not that space travel is possible after all - it is that the first men landing on the moon showed this.

And the conclusion is not that everybody was thrilled - it is that everybody was thrilled when the first men landed on the moon.

But how does this help us find the unstated reasons? I do not think that it does. Not because there is some especially subtle price of reasoning here. No, it is because I do not think that there is any reasoning here at all. The passage can be read as saying, not what *reasons* everybody had for being thrilled, but rather *what they were thrilled at.* So while it looks like an argument, it may not be one.

I am not going to defend this view at any length though. I point it out to those who did not think of it, to stand as it were as a warning:

> Not everything that looks like an argument is an argument.

Exercise 441

Here is my list:

a. London is the capital of France.
b. The violin is a wind instrument.
c. Coffee is a tranquilliser.
d. In Ireland the summer runs from December to February.
e. In Australia they never drink alcohol.
f. People who eat lots of yoghurt live much longer than average.
g. A bullet from a gun goes in a straight line towards its target.
h. There are fifteen vowels and eleven consonants in the alphabet.
i. Germans absolutely refuse to travel.
j. Iron is only half as dense as water.

Exercise 442

Did you manage it every time? It is not cheating to go back and change your first statement if you cannot find a second one. Here is my list:

a. London is not in England.
b. You play a violin by blowing into it.
c. Coffee helps you to go to sleep.
d. In Ireland they have New Year in the summer.
e. In Australia they never get drunk.
f. Yoghurt is particularly good for you.
g. If you want to hit the target you should point the gun straight towards it.
h. There are more vowels than consonants in the alphabet.
i. You are most unlikely to come across a German in Tunisia.
j. Iron will float on water.

Exercise 443

Ice cream contains a lot of vitamins. You see they use starch, which is rich in Vitamins A and B, and sea water which is one of the best sources of Vitamin C.

Exercise 444

In the Antarctic it is warm and sunny all year round, and as you know, plants will not grow in that sort of climate. That's why there are no plants in the Antarctic.

Exercise 445

When you are rich you can get everything you want by simply buying it but when you are poor everything you want is too expensive. That's why rich people are always happier than poor ones.

Exercise 446

Being basically magnetic in their operation, the eyes use up vast quantities of iron. So eating raw carrots gives you amazingly good eyesight, as they are almost entirely made of iron.

Exercise 447

It is an established scientific fact that only those who are perfectly adapted to their environment will survive and breed. That means that we get to know by instinct what it takes to survive. So children usually know what is best for them.

Exercise 448

If you watch a lot of television you will forget how to read. Reading is like swimming - if you do not practice every day you lose the skills entirely. And nobody who watches a lot of television has any chance to practice their reading at all.

Exercise 449

Mathematicians all have exceptionally good eyesight. They need it for doing geometry. And eyesight is the most important thing if you are going to be a musician. So it is easy to learn how to play a musical instrument if you are good at mathematics.

Exercise 450

Lightning never strikes the same place twice. You see, it always strikes the highest object in the vicinity, but when an object gets struck it disappears completely, so something else will then be higher

Reliability   5

This chapter develops techniques for dealing with arguments that are not valid. In particular - a way of working out how *reliable* they are.

As we have defined validity, there is no middle ground between a valid inference and an invalid one. For an inference to be valid the truth of the reasons must guarantee the truth of the conclusion. If there is any possibility, however remote or theoretical, that the conclusion can be false when the reasons are true, then the inference is invalid.

Much of the time though we are not interested in remote or theoretical possibilities. For practical purposes it is frequently safe enough to make an inference, even though, strictly speaking, it is not a valid one.

We need ways of working out just when it is safe to make an inference and when it is not safe. For this purpose we will develop a new concept - *reliability* - which unlike validity is a matter of degree. We will be asking just how reliable an inference is - how safe it is to infer that a conclusion will be true, if we accept that the reasons are also true.

Reliability

So, when we meet an inference the question we ask is this:

> Assuming that the reasons are true, what degree of
> probability would they confer upon the conclusion?

The answer to this question gives the *degree of reliability* of the inference:

Strong	-	If they make it highly probable
Moderate	-	If they make it probable
Weak	-	If they make it improbable

(On this test a valid inference comes out as strongly reliable. Although there is an important theoretical difference between valid inferences and the most strongly reliable of invalid ones, this difference is unimportant in practice. In both cases, if the reasons are true then they make it highly probable that the conclusion will be true.)

In practice, how do we work out these probabilities? The main thing is to be clear that "probable" means *significantly better than chance*. Consider the statement that when I toss a coin it will come up tails. As we all know, a coin cannot be relied upon to do this - it is just as likely to come up heads. We would not say that it is probable that it will come up heads unless we are sure that the chances are much better than even. That is the sense of "probable" to use when working out the reliability of an inference. Imagine that you are betting on the truth of the conclusion. The three grades of reliability more or less equate to these concepts:

Strong	-	A safe bet
Moderate	-	A good bet
Weak	-	A bad bet

Using unstated reasons

The reliability test can always be applied directly, but often it is more straight-forward to use the "unstated reasons" method, asking first what reason or reasons would have to be added to make a valid inference, and then asking how probable it is that these extra reasons are true, given the stated reasons.

> The reliability of an inference equals the
> reliability of the unstated reasons
> (assuming the stated reasons to be true)

Assuming that the stated reasons in an inference are true, the *degree of reliability* of the unstated reasons - and hence of the inference - is:

Strong	-	If it is highly probable that the unstated reasons are true
Moderate	-	If it is probable that the unstated reasons are true
Weak	-	If it is improbable that the unstated reasons are true

When you have made your assessment of the reliability of an inference, write it down, in brackets, alongside the inference line.

Example 1

Starlings cost the farmers a small fortune, as they eat vast quantities of grain.

Marking and constructing the diagram:

1/Starlings cost the farmers a small fortune/, <as> 2/they eat vast quantities of grain/.

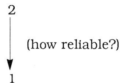

2

(how reliable?)

1

What are the unstated reasons? The main one is that a significant amount of the grain that the starlings (allegedly) eat would otherwise be sold by the farmers for a good price.

What is the probability that this would be true, assuming the stated reason to be true? Well, it would be false in quite a range of conditions: when there is so much grain that the farmers cannot sell all that they grow, when the starlings eat types of grain that the farmers do not grow. And no doubt there are others.

On this basis I would say that even assuming the truth of the stated reason it is improbable that the unstated reason is true, and hence that the inference is weak. And so I write "weak" alongside the inference line:

2

(weak)

1

And there, in one simple diagram, is a clear report on the structure of an argument and on the reliability of the inference.

You will notice that I did not apply the *definition* of "reliable", but used a simpler *test*. Remember the difference between the definition and the test in the case of "valid"? The same goes for "reliable" - it is usually safe to use this test:

> Assuming that the reasons are true, what is the probability that the conclusion is true?

But the test *fails* when the probability of the conclusion is independent of the reasons - when it is conferred upon the conclusion not by the reasons but by something else.

Example 2

> It said on the radio last night that it will be fine today, so we will be able to go to the beach for a picnic after all.

Marking the passage and drawing the diagram:

> 1/It said on the radio last night that it will be fine today/, <so> 2/we will be able to go to the beach for a picnic after all/.

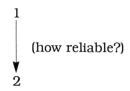

First a little clarification. The statement that we will be able to go to the beach for a picnic is rather ambiguous. At one extreme we might take it to mean that nothing at all is going to prevent us from going, but in the context of this argument it is more reasonable to take it as making the much weaker claim that we are not going to be prevented from going by bad weather. If this were meant to be an argument about factors other than the weather then it should mention them, given the reference to the weather forecast.

Under this interpretation, the unstated reason is: When it says on the radio that the weather will be fine the next day, then it is fine the next day.

In some places, weather forecasts are very reliable, and in others they are wrong quite often. We are not told anything about this in the passage, so we should ask how probable it is, on the average, that the unstated reason is true. Even in the worst cases, it is not probable that it is false - that would require that the forecasters are wrong more often then they are right. And only in the very best cases is it highly probable that the unstated reason is true. So, our "average" judgement is that it is probable but not highly probable that the unstated reason is true, and hence the inference is moderately reliable:

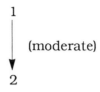

Note how the interpretation bears upon the reliability. If we take the conclusion to mean that nothing at all will prevent us from going to the beach, the inference is much less reliable.

Example 3

> I have added some blue paint to the red paint in this can, so now the paint in the can will be purple.

The structure:

> 1/I have added some blue paint to the red paint in this can/, <so> 2/ <u>now the paint in the can will be purple/</u>.

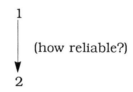

This uses two unstated reasons. The first one is obvious:

> Blue plus red gives purple.

There is another one though:

> Paint plus paint gives paint.

It is highly probable that the second one is true, but it is important that we notice the assumption. As any chemist will tell you, there are plenty of cases where the result of mixing two liquids is more spectacular than a mere change of colour!

So, assuming that it is highly probable that what we get when we mix the blue paint in with the red will be paint, what is the probability that it will turn out to be purple? Anyone who has tried mixing paint will know that producing purple from red and blue is not as easy as you might think. First, if you use only a small amount of red with lots of blue you get blue, and if you use only a small amount of blue with lots of red you get red.

Perhaps we are supposed to assume that the red and blue are in roughly equal quantities? That overcomes the first problem. But then there are the cases where equal quantities of red and blue give not purple but a muddy sort of brownish colour. This happens, so it is certainly possible. If it is only possible, not probable, then the unstated reason is moderately reliable. If it is not only possible but probable then it is weak.

Here I should mention the fact that there will be times when we just do not know. Not everybody knows that when you mix a little black paint with lots of yellow you are quite likely to get a green. On the other hand, there will also no doubt be times when we think we know but don't. For example, plenty of people when asked what happens when you mix red paint with blue unhesitatingly say that you get purple.

Sooner or later, though, we have to make a judgment of the reliability of the inference. My best guess is that it is (just) probable that the added reason is true, and so the inference is moderately reliable. But it is close going - it just scrapes in as "moderate".

Here is the verdict:

1

(moderate)

2

A tactical point

There are many cases where an inference is not valid but it is difficult to say what has to be added to produce a valid inference - the unstated reasons are not at all easy to state. If you have this trouble, there is a purely mechanical method you can use for beefing up the reasons to make an inference valid. If the reasons are (collectively) R and the conclusion is C, then you can add the extra reason "If R then C" and (Hey Presto!) the conclusion follows validly. By doing this we produce an argument of the Modus Ponens form:

$$\text{If R then C}$$
$$\text{R}$$
$$\text{Therefore C}$$

and arguments of this form have to be valid.

That is the good news. Now for the bad news: First, the extra reason we add with this method will be particular rather than general, in that any names etc that appear in the reasons R or the conclusion C will remain. And we do not want that. For example, in Exercise 501 (below) the extra reason should not mention Mary or Sue by name. And second, when it comes to deciding whether the inference is reliable, what we have done is simply replace the question whether R —►C is a *reliable* inference with the question whether, in the light of the stated reason R, "If R then C" is *probable*. And that is hardly progress.

But still, if all else fails, it is a good idea to start this way and see what happens.

Model Answers

Do not be alarmed if you have judged an inference "moderate" when I have judged it "weak", etc. Make sure though that we differ only on how probable some unstated reason is, not on what the unstated reasons are. If your unstated reasons are not the same as mine, make sure that I am the one that is mistaken. If not, see if you can do better the next time - try to improve your "logical imagination" as you do these exercises.

EXERCISE FIVE

Draw a structure diagram of the reasoning in each of these passages.
Work out how reliable each inference is. Write this on the diagram, alongside the inference line.
Use the "unstated reasons" method wherever you can.
Explain your answers fully.

501 Mary always beats Pamela at tennis, and Pamela always beats Sue. So Mary has to beat Sue.

502 It is a good idea to learn about other cultures. That way you come to realise how lucky you are.

503 Tina prefers pastels to strong colours. See, she's wearing pale pink, and her room is done in peach and dove grey.

504 The statistics show that there are fewer accidents in countries which do not allow the consumption of alcohol. So we should ban it outright.

505 This cannot be a genuine Picasso. It is signed, and he never signed his work.

506 This is why the movies can be so gripping in their presentation of man: they do not give us his thoughts as novels have done for so long, but his conduct or behaviour. They directly present to us that special way of being in the world, of dealing with things and other people, which we can see in the sign language of gesture and gaze and which clearly defines each person we know.

507 Mary does not eat meat any more. She has become a Buddhist, and they are not allowed meat.

508 You want to know why he's a thief? Because he's a thief, that's why - he's just a thief.

509 Tomato plants should be tied onto stakes. It keeps the fruit off the ground.

510 Uneconomic farms must be merged without delay. The amount of labour and machinery needed would immediately be reduced, and better quality could be used in both areas without overtaxing either training programmes or manufacturing capacity.

511 Plato maintained that knowledge of the everyday mundane world is not true knowledge, as this world is a mere shadow or reflection of the true world, the World of Forms.

512 If you really want to get ahead in your job you will have to stop arguing with your boss. Despite what she says, she really does prefer yes-men. Look at the ones who have been promoted and you will see that I am right.

513 Do not use that chisel as a screwdriver. You will ruin the cutting edge and it will never be any good as a chisel again.

514 The Mosaic Law of the Jews forbade them to eat any fish without scales, so they had to do without eels.

515 Six is divisible by three and four is divisible by two so ten is divisible by five.

---

516 The Volga river flows through Auckland and on through Mexico City to the sea. So Auckland must be higher than Mexico City.

517 It is usually very windy in the tropics. The constant hot weather produces large static anticyclones, and they have a lot of isobars close together, so you get strong winds all the time.

518 You must let Mary have the bean chair, Stephen - she got here first and that's the one she wants.

519 The Cubans are a taciturn and reserved people. Like the Hungarians they have a dictatorial government, and like the Italians they live in isolation on an island.

520 Being unable to see, bats have to use a form of radar to avoid obstacles when flying.

521 Oh dear, Uncle Fred's going to sing! He's had too much to drink and you know that he always bursts into song when he's tipsy.

522 You cannot have that. It is mine.

523 Compared with the smaller shops, a supermarket has an enormous turnover, and so you know that everything you buy there will be fresh.

524 That was Bob Geldof walking passed. I saw his photo in last night's paper and I never forget a face.

525 There is no need to use a special primer or undercoat when you use one of the new acrylic paints, so your paint job will last just as long if you do it all in acrylic.

526 Of course he was the one that robbed the bank. Some of the money was found in his room, and there were running shoes and a stocking mask there too.

527 There will not be any sea breeze today. It is 2.30 in the afternoon and still dead calm, and everyone knows that if it doesn't come in by 2pm it won't come in at all.

528 You shouldn't ever eat bananas - they are really bad for you. You see they contain a lot of calcium and that ruins your teeth. And remember they come from tropical countries where there are all sorts of exotic diseases.

529 This one will not let you down - all of the cars we sell are reliable.

530 Unless you want to be an engineer it is a waste of time to learn mathematics. Nowadays we can use computers to do all of the tedious calculations.

531 You will never become a great middle distance runner, Tony. All of the top runners have abnormally low resting heartbeat rates, and yours is just average.

532 Potatoes should be planted in clumps rather than rows. That way the windflows are broken and the plants shelter one another and so the insects cannot attack them.

533 I have not had a toothache for two or three years, so I will be able to go with you on your long trekking expedition without having to worry about my teeth.

534 There has been no fighting in the Middle East for three years now, and all of the diseases have been wiped out, so we will be able to have that holiday in Iran without having to worry at all.

535 The West Germans have more cars per head than anyone else, which shows that West Germany is the wealthiest country in the world.

536 It never snows in Africa. To start with there is almost no water there, and anyway it is far too hot for snow.

537 Japan is by no means a wealthy country. They have fewer personal computers per head than almost any developed nation.

538 There is no need to check the oil level in a motor. They run perfectly well with next to no oil in the sump, and anyway if the oil is running low the warning light comes on.

539 You should wait a while before buying yourself a computer - prices have been dropping steadily for three years now, so they are sure to be even cheaper by this time next year.

540 Napoleon was born in 1795 - his mother was thirty-six when he was born and she was born in 1761. And he was fifty-four at the Battle of Waterloo. So that must have been in 1856.

EXERCISE FIVE - MODEL ANSWERS

Exercise 501

1/Mary always beats Pamela at tennis/, and 2/Pamela always beats Sue/. <So> 3/<u>Mary has to beat Sue</u>/.

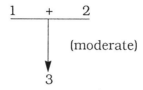

This one may *sound* better than "moderate", but the argument assumes that

If A beats B and B beats C then A will beat C.

This is a fairly safe bet, but by no means a certainty. In our terms, it is probable but not highly probable that it is true. Mary may beat Pamela who is unable to return her fast serve, and Pamela may beat Sue who cannot read her deceptive top spin, but Sue still beats Mary, returning her serve comfortably and getting in for the volley. If, as I believe, this sort of case is possible but not probable (that is it is distinctly more probable that if A beats B and B beats C then A will beat C) then the inference is moderately reliable.

Exercise 502

1/<u>It is a good idea to learn about other cultures.</u> <That way> 2/you come to realise how lucky you are/.

This is complicated by the fact that there are two interpretations of the reason. On one reading it means find out *whether* you are very lucky, or very unlucky. But the more likely interpretation is, *realise* that you *are* very lucky. That is how I am interpreting it for the "weak" verdict. Under this interpretation the counterexamples include the people who find out how *unlucky* they are by learning about other cultures - people in underprivileged countries. I suspect that they outnumber the ones who find out how *lucky* they are, and if that is so then the inference is a poor one.

Exercise 503

1/Tina prefers pastels to strong colours/. See, 2/she's wearing pale pink/, and 3/her room is done in peach and dove grey/.

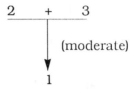

First question: Did Tina choose these colours? Answer: We have no way of telling. Solution: Assume that she did?

We could be hard-hearted and say that one of the unstated reasons is that people choose their own colours, but it strikes me that only a rather illogical person would offer the reasons given here as reasons for someone's preferences if there was more than a remote possibility that it was not a matter of choice. And I think that it is reasonable to assume that the arguer is reasonably logical, not rather illogical.

So, I am going to accept that Tina chose these colours. Given that, what unstated reasons are there?

Notice that only two examples of her choices are mentioned. Maybe she rides a vivid red motorbike and only wears her pastel coloured clothes to work to please the boss, wearing vibrant colours the rest of the time. The unstated reason is that these are typical of the colours she chooses. And here, I do not think that we should be quite so forgiving. It is certainly possible that this unstated reason is false. I doubt that it is probable - if she was the one who chose the peach and pale grey scheme for her room it is a fairly good bet that these are typical of her colour preferences.

So, I would rate the unstated reason as probable but not highly probable, and so the inference rates as moderately reliable.

Note though that again it was perhaps a close decision. All this detailed working out is necessary, even if we do end up with an unexciting verdict.

Exercise 504

The statistics show that 1/there are fewer accidents in countries which do not allow the consumption of alcohol/. <So> 2/we should ban it outright/.

1

(weak)

2

It is important to omit the first four words from 1. It is not because the statistics show that there are fewer accidents that we should ban alcohol. The reason is that there *are* fewer accidents.

Again the inference is not a good one. We must look for scenarios in which the reason is true and in which banning alcohol would not be a good idea, and the USA during prohibition comes to mind. Is it worthwhile running the risk of organised gang activity, sly-grogging etc, so as to reduce the road toll by an as yet unstated amount? (Even allowing, that is, that the connection is a causal one, which is not established in the argument.) No, we would want better reasons than that . And the scenario I describe is likely enough, not a science fiction fantasy. So the inference is weak.

Exercise 505

> 1/This cannot be a genuine Picasso. / - 2/It is signed/, and 3/he never signed his work/.

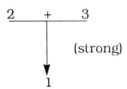

2   +   3

(strong)

1

Here the direct approach is best. Ask - Assuming these reasons to be true, is it possible for the conclusion to be false? And the answer is that this is most unlikely. Unless somebody has forged a signature on a genuine Picasso, the conclusion will be true.

In this exercise we must not be put off by what I am fairly sure is a false reason. I am sure I have seen Picasso's signature on his (allegedly genuine) works. But that is not the point. Our task at this stage is only to find out if the conclusion follows, not whether the reasons are true. Certainly, any argument containing a false statement must be unsound, but it can still be valid.

Exercise 506

<This is why> 1/<u>the movies can be so gripping in their presentation of man</u>/: 2/they do not give us his thoughts as novels have done for so long, but his conduct or behaviour/. 3/They directly present to us that special way of being in the world, of dealing with things and other people, which we can see in the sign language of gesture and gaze and which clearly defines each person we know/.

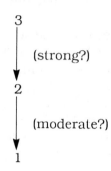

You may prefer to treat 3 as an expanded version of 2 rather than a reason for it, in which case your diagram will be simpler.

Treating 3 as a reason for 2, I want to say that the inference is a strong one, 3 spelling out what it means to present conduct rather than thoughts, but on the other hand I am not entirely clear what any of this means, and that makes an assessment very difficult. Hence my doubts.

The move from 2 to 1 is no easier to assess. The conclusion as worded expresses only a possibility - the movies do not often have to do this for the conclusion to be true. Indeed, interpreted as merely stating a possibility, the conclusion seems to be true anyway, independently of whether the reason is true. If that is so then according to our test the inference is valid.

But wait - that is a silly result. Why should we say that the inference is valid just because its conclusion is always true? Shouldn't the reason play some part? Of course it should. This is why our definition of "valid" states that an inference is valid when the truth of the reasons would guarantee the truth of the conclusion. Other independent guarantees are beside the point. So here we have one of the cases where the test may fail, where we have to use the definition.

Of course it is probably a mistake to take the words "can be" literally, in the conclusion. And if we take it as saying that the movies often *are* gripping, it is easy enough to think of circumstances in which the conclusion is false.

Whether the reason can at the same time be true is another question - it depends upon what the reason means, which is not entirely clear.

Exercise 507

1/Mary does not eat meat any more/. 2/She has become a Buddhist/ and 3/they are not allowed meat/.

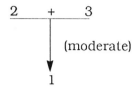

The unstated reason has to provide some link between not being allowed to do something and not doing it. The most general statement:

People do not do what they are not allowed to do.

If we were really fussy we might change this so that it is only about females. Either way, there are plenty of exceptions, so the inference is not strongly reliable. On the other hand, the exceptions will be a fairly small minority, I should think. If that is so, then it is probable but not highly probable that the unstated reason is true, and so the inference is moderately reliable.

Exercise 508

You want to know why 1/he's a thief/? <Because> 1/he's a thief/, that's why - he's just a thief.

According to the test for validity, we can validly infer any statement from itself. If the statement - the reason - is true, there is no way in which the same statement - the conclusion - can be false. On the other hand, according to the definition of "valid" this is not a good inference: the truth of 1, if guaranteed by anything, must surely be guaranteed by something other than 1.

What are we to do? Rate the inference as "weak"? Even that does not feel quite right, and the reason is that, although the passage is written in the form of an argument, it does not have to be read as an argument at all. Indeed, it is perhaps best read as a refusal to argue, a denial that there are any further reasons. And that is my final verdict on this - it is not an argument at all, and so questions of reliability do not arise.

Exercise 509

1/Tomato plants should be tied onto stakes/ - 2/it keeps the fruit off the ground/.

One unstated reason is that the tomatoes are being grown to produce good fruit. It is highly probable that this is true. Another is that the fruit will not be good unless they are kept off the ground. Again, it is highly probable that this is true.

But there is another, much less reliable unstated reason: That the best way to keep them off the ground is to tie them onto stakes. In fact there are plenty of other ways, ways which are in fact commonly used, that are perfectly acceptable as alternatives to stakes. So it is not only possible that stakes are not the best way to keep them off the ground - it is probable, and the inference is only weakly reliable.

Note that we have been taking the reason to be saying that tomatoes should be tied onto stakes rather than wires or strings etc. Another interpretation is that they should be tied onto stakes or anything else that will do the same job. On that interpretation, the inference is much more reliable.

Exercise 510

1/Uneconomic farms must be merged without delay/. 2/The amount of labour and machinery needed would immediately be reduced/, and 3/better quality could be used in both areas without overtaxing either training programmes or manufacturing capacity/.

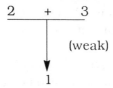

I have diagrammed this as linked because there seems to be some sort of connection between the two reasons. I cannot say exactly what this connection is, because I know next to nothing about agriculture. Why then do I boldly declare the inference to be weak? Because I need to know far more than the technicalities before accepting this sort of conclusion. From an economic point of view it might be a good idea to merge the farms, for the reasons stated, but it could be disastrous socially. The reference to a reduction in labour requirements suggests that this might well be so.

Note that the terms "true" and "probable" do not apply very happily to this sort of example. When you find that this is the case I think that it is wise to press on intuitively, as it were, asking whether and to what extent the reasons render the conclusion acceptable. Indeed there is a whole new theoretical framework that could be spelled out here. In this example, I do not believe that the reasons stated, even if true, contribute very much to the acceptability of the conclusion, which may be entirely unacceptable for other reasons. That is why I have said that the inference is weak.

Exercise 511

Plato maintained that 1/knowledge of the everyday mundane world is not true knowledge/, <as> 2/this world is a mere shadow or reflection of the true world, the World of Forms/.

I have left out the opening words, because it seems to me that the conclusion is about knowledge, not Plato. My main reason for this is that the reason is not about Plato. If the stated reason started with the words "he believed that", I would include the words "Plato maintained that" in the conclusion.

The unstated reason is that knowledge of a shadow or reflection of something is not true knowledge of that thing. Now we must grant that often this is so. But how often? Is it ever possible that we can achieve true knowledge of something through its shadow or reflection? Of course this is sometimes possible. My dentist uses a mirror to see what is going on inside my tooth. Surely he is coming to know, truly, about the hole he is drilling?

So it is possible that the unstated reason is false. If it were only about shadows

I would rate this as a fairly low probability, but I can think of all sorts of cases where we use reflections to obtain accurate information, and so I think that it is not only possible but also probable that this is false. It is improbable that it is true. The inference, accordingly, is weak.

Notice how you did not have to know anything at all about Plato to evaluate this inference (which is not really surprising, as it is not really about Plato).

Exercise 512

If 1/you really want to get ahead in your job/ [<so>] 2/you will have to stop arguing with your boss/. Despite what she says, 3/she really does prefer yes-men/. 4/Look at the ones who have been promoted and you will see that I am right/.

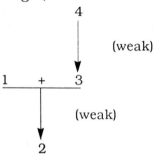

Perhaps it is a little unfair to diagram 4 as reason for 3, because 4 only says that there is evidence for 3 - it does not state the evidence. And this hardly contributes at all to the probability of 3. After all, there can be some evidence for all manner of unlikely yarns.

Note that I have split up an "If ... then .." sentence. Here I am confident that although the hypothetical form is used, what is meant is that you do want to get ahead and so you will have to stop arguing.

At first sight the inference from 1 plus 3 to 2 looks good. But wait - who said that the boss gets what she wants? Perhaps her daughter really runs the show, or her bank manager, or her astrologer? So again, an inference which looks fine turns out to have plenty of counterexamples, and quite likely ones at that.

Exercise 513

1/Do not use that chisel as a screwdriver/. 2/You will ruin the cutting edge/ and 3/it will never be any good as a chisel again/.

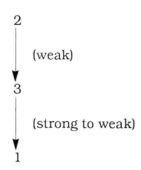

2

(weak)

3

(strong to weak)

1

The inference from 2 to 3 assumes that chisels that are ruined cannot be fixed. Of course there is a sense of "ruined" where this is more or less true by definition, but I doubt that that is appropriate here. In this case, as far as I know, all that has to be done to unruin a chisel is to sharpen it again. If that is so - and it is certainly the case that many other ruined items can be repaired - then it is improbable that the unstated reason is true, and so the inference is only weak.

Note that if we take the unstated reason to be more general - that things that are ruined cannot be fixed, not just about chisels - then the probabilities may come out differently. It is a straightforward matter to fix a chisel that has been ruined, but many other things are likely to be ruined beyond repair, when they are ruined. This shows the importance of getting the unstated reasons right. This argument is about chisels only.

The other inference, from 3 to 1, assumes that the chisel cannot be spared. The reliability of this sort of inference is very hard to assess: if there are plenty of chisels and no screwdrivers then the unstated reason is probably false, but if there are plenty of screwdrivers and only the one chisel it is probably true. Now, the first of these scenarios gives a reliability of "weak", while the second a reliability of "strong", and as I do not think that we have any good reason for choosing one rather than the other, I have indicated this range of reliabilities on the diagram. This gives a clear indication of what is going on.

Exercise 514

1/The Mosaic Law of the Jews forbade them to eat any fish without scales/, <so> 2/they had to do without eels/.

1

(weak)

2

My information is that, if the (Biblical) Jews did believe that eels have no scales, they certainly would have been mistaken in that belief, as eels do have tiny scales. So a rule against scaleless fish lends no support at all to the conclusion that one must forgo eels, even though one might understandably believe that it does.

I am not of course suggesting that the ancient Jews used this argument. And the reasoning would be much better if it included a statement that eels do not have scales. (As is so often the case, you can improve your logic by departing from the truth.) But that is not in the argument we have been presented with.

Exercise 515

> 1/Six is divisible by three/ and 2/four is divisible by two/ <so> 3/ten is divisible by five/.

If it is to have any plausibility at all, this argument has to be seen as first supporting and then using an unstated reason - 4 - such as:

> If A is divisible by X and B is divisible by Y then A plus B is divisible by X plus Y.

But while 1, 2 and 3 conform to this pattern, the formula is not a truth of arithmetic:

> 15 is divisible by 3, and 4 is divisible by 2; but 19 is not divisible by 5.

Of course we may have got the wrong formula for 4, and there are other candidates, some of them interesting.

Exercise 516

> 1/The Volga river flows through Auckland and on through Mexico City to the sea/. <So> 2/Auckland must be higher than Mexico City/

This is like the paint-mixing example and the arithmetical one - for there to be any connection at all between the reason and the conclusion there has to be an extra reason, which takes the form of a "rule". Here it would have to be to the effect that rivers flow only from higher places to lower ones.

And for counterexamples, we have to look for exceptions to the rule. In the other cases we have met they abound. Here, though they are logically possible they are not empirically possible. They are therefore most unlikely, and the inference is a strong one.

Exercise 517

> 1/It is usually very windy in the tropics/. 2/The constant hot weather produces large static anticyclones/, and 3/they have a lot of isobars close together/, <so> 1/you get strong winds all the time/.

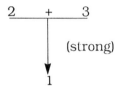

I have regarded the last statement as a repetition of the first one. Strictly speaking they do not say the same thing - "all the time" is stronger than "usually" - but I doubt that there are two conclusions being argued for in a simple passage like this.

To forge a link between the (false) statement about the isobars (in an anticyclone) being close together and windiness we need to add a statement to the effect that these are connected.

And it turns out that this, unlike the reasons that have actually been stated, is true. So the inference is strongly reliable, despite the falsehood of the stated reasons.

A note on straightforwardly true and on straightforwardly false statements. If an unstated reason is true, it is at least highly probable that it is true, and so it is strongly reliable. If it is false, it is (totally) improbable that it is true, and so the inference it supports is weak.

Exercise 518

> 1/You must let Mary have the bean chair, Stephen/ - 2/she got here first/ and 3/that's the one she wants/.

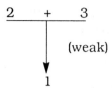

Look for conditions in which she did get there first and does want to sit in the bean chair, but should not be allowed to do so. There are several: The beanchair is Stephen's not hers; She has a bad back and must sit in a hard upright chair; It is Stephen's turn; She promised Stephen the bean chair; and so on. These are commonplace, expectable conditions, and so the inference is weak.

Exercise 519

> 1/The Cubans are a taciturn and reserved people/. 2/Like the Hungarians they have a dictatorial government/, and 3/like the Italians they live in isolation on an island/.

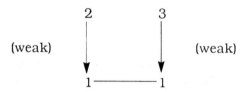

Unstated reasons: A dictatorial government or living on an island makes you taciturn and/or reserved.

I find it as easy to think of counterexamples as to think of supporting examples, in both cases, and so it is improbable that either unstated reason is true. Hence, both inferences are weak.

Exercise 520

> <Being> 1/unable to see/, 2/bats have to use a form of radar to avoid obstacles when flying/.

It helps to rewrite the first sentences as - "<As> 1/they are unable to see/".

People who know about bats are tempted to complain that it is not the case that bats cannot see. But remember that it does not matter, as far as the inference is concerned, whether or not the reason is true. What matters is the extent to which, if it were true, it would support the conclusion. And here there is little support. There is really nothing in the argument to say that a blind creature could avoid obstacles when flying only by using something like radar. And indeed, what bats use is like sonar rather than radar, so it is entirely possible that the conclusion be true while the reason is false, and so the inference is weak.

Exercise 521

Oh dear, 1/Uncle Fred's going to sing/! 2/He's had too much to drink/ and you know that 3/he always bursts into song when he's tipsy/.

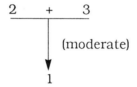

Not quite valid - he may be able to take too much alcohol without getting tipsy (for example he may often just go to sleep). But it is not very far from being valid. If we were to change the last words of the passage so that it says "when he's had too much to drink" then it would be valid, and that is not a very radical change, although the dedicated and serious drinkers will disagree with me here.

As it stands I would say that the unstated reason - that people get tipsy when they have too much (alcohol) to drink - is likely. But plenty of people fall down unconscious or go berserk, and unless you are prepared to count these as cases of "tipsy" too, the unstated reason is no more than likely, and so the inference is no more than moderately reliable.

Exercise 522

1/You cannot have that/. 2/It is mine/.

Although we often accept this line or reasoning, it is as it stands no good at all. Consider this counterargument

> Yes, you can have that. It is mine.

We often accept that line of reasoning too. Odd! The reason is the same, but the conclusions contradict one another.

In each case, for the inference to be acceptably strong we need to add further reasons, to the effect that I am entitled to say who can have something which is mine, plus a statement that I have decided that you can, or cannot, as the case may be.

Even if we accept the general principle that I am entitled to say who can have something of mine, that on its own does not make either inference a strong one. We also need to know whether or not permission has been granted. If that is not settled, neither inference is strong, as it might well be settled either way.

Exercise 523

> 1/Compared with the smaller shops, a supermarket has an enormous turnover/, <and so> you know that 2/everything you buy there will be fresh/.

I prefer to treat phrases like "you know that" as rhetorical. Of course sometimes they will not be, but here I would be surprised if anyone were arguing for a conclusion about what I know rather than how fresh the supermarket's goods are. Of course if the intended conclusion is that I know, then the one I have marked also follows. "I know that p" entails "p", but of course "p" does not entail "I know that p".

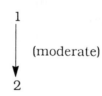

There is no strong connection between the reason and the conclusion. Perhaps there is a reasonable link between having a higher turnover and having fresher stock, but that is not what the argument says. If the stock in the corner dairy is really unfresh the supermarket's stock does not have to be fresh to be fresher than that. One unstated reason is that new stock will be fresh stock. Likely, perhaps, but not certain.

Also, the argument assumes that a high turnover ensures a fresh stock, and while we would hope that that is true, we know only too well that there are exceptions - where the new stock is placed in front of old stock on the shelves, and so on. Again, the unstated reason is no more than plain likely. Remember that the conclusion refers to everything you buy in the supermarket. And so, as so often, the inference turns out no better than "moderate".

Exercise 524

1/That was Bob Geldof walking passed/. 2/I saw his photo in last night's paper/ and 3/I never forget a face/.

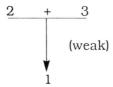

The reasons are true and the conclusion is false if the person walking past is a Geldof lookalike. There only has to be one lookalike for the chances that it is Geldof himself to be only one in two. I am told that it is highly likely that there is at least one Geldof lookalike, and so I have rated the inference as weak.

Exercise 525

1/There is no need to use a special primer or undercoat when you use one of the new acrylic paints/, <so> 2/your paint job will last just as long if you do it all in acrylic/.

Were you tempted to say this one is moderate? I was for a moment. But think - the reason is only that there is no need to use a primer or undercoat. All that that guarantees, if true, is that the paint will not fall off more or less straight away. That is well short of saying that the paint will last for as long as a traditional job with all the proper undercoats. So the conclusion can easily be false while the reason is true - if the paint job lasts even an hour less without an undercoat or primer.

Exercise 526

<Of course> 1/he was the one that robbed the bank/. 2/Some of the money was found in his room/, and 3/there were running shoes and a stocking mask there too/.

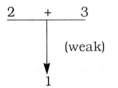

Counterexamples are highly likely: It may have been his room mate who robbed the bank, and so on.

Exercise 527

1/There will not be any sea breeze today/. 2/It is 2.30 in the afternoon and still dead calm/, and everyone knows that 3/if it doesn't come in by 2pm it won't come in at all/.

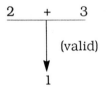

I treat "everyone knows that" as a rhetorical flourish. You may leave it in, though, because if everyone does know this then it follows that it is true.

There cannot be any counterexamples here. The reasons completely rule out any possibility that the conclusion is false.

For those who like jargon, this is an example of the traditional valid form of argument called *Modus Ponens*, which you met in Chapter Four. (For those who do not like jargon - there is no point in remembering phrases like that, unless you want to impress people with your erudition.)

Exercise 528

1/You shouldn't ever eat bananas/ - 2/they are really bad for you/. <You see> 3/they contain a lot of calcium/ and 4/that ruins your teeth/And remember 5/they come from tropical countries where there are all sorts of exotic diseases/.

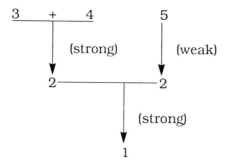

I was tempted to mark the dash as an inference word.

Don't be sidetracked by the falsity of some of the reasons. If bananas did contain lots of calcium and if that did ruin your teeth, then that would make it highly likely that they are bad for you. The only counterexamples would be when bananas also contain some vital substance not obtainable elsewhere and which is destroyed if you try to remove the calcium.

The inference from 5 to 2 is a poor one. There are all sorts of exotic diseases in a hospital too but that does not mean that I am likely to catch them if I go there.

Exercise 529

1/This one will not let you down/ - 2/all of the cars we sell are reliable/

Strictly, as stated the inference rates only as "weak". Until we are told that this is one of the cars we sell the reason does not even start to support the conclusion. Did you notice that unstated reason?

Ignoring that, the inference is much better, but still only moderate, not valid. The argument still assumes that a reliable car will not let you down, which is not strictly true. Granted, if it lets you down often it is not reliable, but a car can be reliable and still occasionally let you down.

Exercise 530

1/Unless you want to be an engineer it is a waste of time to learn mathematics/. 2/Nowadays we can use computers to do all of the tedious calculations/.

If the only reason one could have for learning mathematics was to perform calculations then the argument might have some force, but as many mathematicians will insist, mathematics is more than mere number crunching. So, unless all these other facets of mathematics are a waste of time, the argument is a poor one.

Exercise 531

1/You will never become a great middle distance runner, Tony/. 2/ All of the top runners have abnormally low resting heartbeat rates/, and 3/yours is just average/.

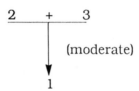

Two main fields for counterexamples come to mind: Tony turns out to be the first great middle-distance runner with an average resting heartbeat rate; and Tony finds a way of reducing his rate and goes on to become one of the greats. My hunch is that these are both unlikely. Hence my rating of "moderate". And note how, by admitting that it is based on a hunch, I can easily change it later. Persuade me to change my hunch and of course I will change my rating too.

Exercise 532

1/Potatoes should be planted in clumps rather than rows/. 2/That way the windflows are broken/ and 3/the plants shelter one another/ <and so> 4/the insects cannot attack them/.

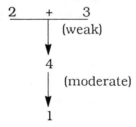

I cannot see any connection at all between the alleged shelter and the ability of insects to attack potatoes. But if the insects are prevented from attacking, that is a fairly good reason for planting in rows. Of course it might be outweighed by reasons against - ease of cultivation, perhaps - but it does make the conclusion probable.

You may have diagrammed this as a single long chain? That is an acceptable interpretation of the passage.

Exercise 533

> 1/I have not had a toothache for two or three years/, <so> 2/<u>I will be able to go with you on your long trekking expedition without having to worry about my teeth</u>/.

I am taking the conclusion to mean "without having any trouble with my teeth". This is not what it literally says, and it makes the argument weaker, but I'm sure that it is what would be meant by any reasonable person using these words.

Given that, the inference is not at all good. I know that I can go for several years or more without toothache and then something goes wrong, and I think there are lots like me. So it is likely that the reason is true while the conclusion is false - the inference is weak.

Exercise 534

> 1/There has been no fighting in the Middle East for three years now/ and 2/all of the diseases have been wiped out/, <so> 3/<u>we will be able to have that holiday in Iran without having to worry at all</u>/.

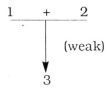

If the conclusion means only that we will be able to go on holiday without having to worry about fighting and disease, the inference is not entirely hopeless. But a three year lull in fighting is not an eternal peace, and it may be impossible for holiday makers to get into Iran. So even on the most charitable interpretation this is a weak inference. And when the conclusion it taken literally the inference is dreadful. There is a host of other perils that the reasons do not rule out.

Exercise 535

1/The West Germans have more cars per head than anyone else/, <which shows that> 2/West Germany is the wealthiest country in the world/.

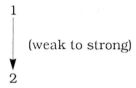

This argument assumes that the number of cars per head is a certain sign of wealth. But that is not so - they must also be high quality cars, surely, and the argument does not state that. So as it stands it is only weak.

If, though, you think that this goes without saying - that it is common knowledge that the West Germans typically have superior cars - then you might want to regard this as a simple omission from the passage, in which case the rating is "strong".

Exercise 536

1/It never snows in Africa/. To start with 2/there is almost no water there/and anyway 3/it is far too hot for snow/.

I am taking the expression "and anyway" to indicate that the two reasons are independent - that even if the first turns out to be mistaken, the second is sufficient. Hence the diagram.

The inference from 3 to 1 is a very reliable one. If it is too hot for snow it will not snow. That could be added as the unstated reason, and it is very highly probable. (But not all such statements are: cf "If he is too old to jog he will not jog".)

The other inference is not as good. A small amount of water could give a small amount of snow.

Exercise 537

> 1/Japan is by no means a wealthy country/. 2/They have fewer personal computers per head than almost any developed nation/.

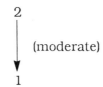

This is rather like the one about cars, except this time it is harder to bring in considerations of quality. The argument assumes that the number of personal computers per head is an accurate measure of wealth, for a developed nation. And that is quite close to the truth, I am told. So the inference is moderately reliable.

Do not be put off by the fact that neither the reason nor the conclusion is true.

Exercise 538

> 1/There is no need to check the oil level in a motor/. 2/They run perfectly well with next to no oil in the sump/, and anyway 3/if the oil is running low the warning light comes on/.

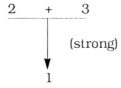

The phrase "and anyway" may suggest to you that these are independent reasons. If so, diagram as convergent.

As I have diagrammed it (being not convinced that it is convergent), this is a highly reliable inference. Even ignoring 2 altogether, if the warning light is a reliable guide then there is no need to check (with the dipstick).

Exercise 539

1/<u>You should wait a while before buying yourself a computer</u>/ - 2/ prices have been dropping steadily for three years now/, <so> 3/they are sure to be even cheaper by this time next year/.

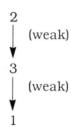

Divide and rule is the rule - take them one by one. The inference from 2 to 3 is weak because there is nothing in 2 to rule out the possibility - by no means remote - that prices have "bottomed out". And the inference from 3 to 1 is weak because there is nothing in the argument to persuade us that price is even an important consideration, let alone the overriding one. For example, the need for a computer may be so urgent that it would be foolish to wait for a (possible) further drop in price.

Exercise 540

1/Napoleon was born in 1795/ - 2/his mother was thirty-six when he was born/ and 3/she was born in 1761/. And 4/he was fifty-four at the Battle of Waterloo/. <So> 5/<u>that must have been in 1856</u>/.

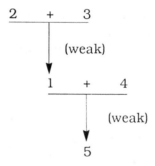

61 plus 36 is not 95, and so on, and that effects the inferences. You might simply take the false arithmetic propositions used to be the unstated reasons.

Note too that even if 61 plus 36 were 95, the inference which uses it would still not be any good. He might have been born just before she turned 37, etc.

Divide and Rule   6

The methods we have been using to determine the reliability of an inference apply, of course, to each of the inferences in a complex argument. In practice, though, it can be tedious and often pointless to attend to every move in an argument, when there are a great number of them. What we can do is decide whether some of the inferences are more important than the others, and attend to them first.

Often - perhaps even usually - the final inference is the most important in a complex argument. But this is by no means always the case. So unless we are prepared to play safe and examine all of the inferences, we will have to work out which is the most important conclusion. The inference or inferences which lead to that statement will be the ones to start on. Of course if those inferences turn out to be reliable, we must continue looking for weaknesses, elsewhere in the argument, and we may end up having to examine all of the inferences in detail. There is no guarantee that there will be a short-cut. After all, even if all of the inferences in an argument are strong, we are going to have to look at all of them to find this out.

Different sorts of argument structure call for different approaches. In the case of a chain argument, start with the inference which leads to the main conclusion. If that inference is rejected as faulty then the rest of the argument can safely be ignored - the conclusion is not well supported even if the other inferences in the chain are impeccable. A chain argument is no stronger than its weakest link.

On the other hand, when an inference is convergent the conclusion can be well supported even if one of the inferences is no good at all. As the inferences lead independently to the conclusion, only one of them has to be strong. Here, there is no chain for a weak link to break.

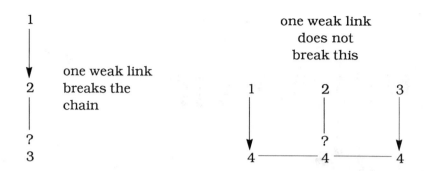

An example

You shouldn't drink so much beer, Mike. You know that it makes you put on weight and already your best jacket is too tight for you. Anyway you cannot afford to spend so much on drink - you're passed your overdraft limit already.

First we mark the passage in the usual way:

1/You shouldn't drink so much beer, Mike/. You know that 2/it makes you put on weight/ and 3/already your best jacket is too tight for you/Anyway 4/you cannot afford to spend so much on drink/ - 5/ you're past your overdraft limit already/.

The diagram goes like this:

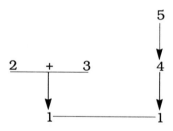

First, let me illustrate the "Divide and Rule" rule. The argument breaks down into these three parts, which can be treated separately:

You can see that even if the inference from 2 + 3 to 1 is a weak one, 1 may turn out to be well supported by 4. And that even if 5 is not a good reason for 4 it would be silly to criticise the whole argument on that basis. After all, the argument could easily be improved, simply by eliminating 5 and hence also the inference from 5 to 4! So, here there are two equally prominent inferences - only one of which needs to be a good one - and a third inference which does not matter very much.

As an argument becomes more and more complex the job of assessing it as a whole does tend to become longer and longer but it does not have to become complex or even difficult. The title of this chapter is meant to remind us of the key move:

> DIVIDE AND RULE!

That is:

> Treat the separate inferences separately.
> Treat the most important inferences first.

To do this:

> Ask - What is the main conclusion?
> Ask - What is its main line of support?
> Ask - How well is it supported?

If you manage to expose a fatal flaw, or even a major one, you can stop. So sometimes you can deal with a long and complex argument very quickly indeed. (But remember that an unreliable inference may not be a fatal flaw in an argument - the structure matters also.)

Extended arguments

Often the arguments you have to deal with are found in articles or whole books rather than in short passages. The first move here is to construct an accurate summary of the argument. Start by deciding what is the chief conclusion, then work out what are the most central and direct reasons stated for (and/or against) this conclusion, and so on. Much of this will have to be in your own words. Try to state all of the main reasons and conclusions in a single short passage, which can then be dealt with in the usual way. Any particularly difficult or complex argument can be dealt with separately.

Drawing diagrams

Some people have difficulty drawing structure diagrams for complex passages. Here is a suggestion.

When you have decided what are the reasons and conclusions, rewriting them if necessary, take a fresh sheet of paper and write the number of the conclusion at the bottom. Then draw an arrow pointing down to the conclusion.

Now decide what is the main reason supporting that conclusion, and write its number at the top of the arrow.

Next, decide whether it stands alone or is linked with another reason - if the latter write a plus sign and the number of that reason.

Now draw another arrow pointing down to the main conclusion, and look for further reasons which support it directly. If there are none, rub it out.

Go on to look for reasons supporting the reasons you have already represented on your diagram. And so on, moving up the page.

Working this way from the bottom up is by far the best way to proceed, and using a whole sheet of paper for working out a structure may waste a little paper but it often saves a lot of time and anguish.

EXERCISE SIX

Assess the reasoning in the following passages.
If you judge one inference to be more important than another, say why.
If you can think of any "rules" - like the "Divide and Rule" rule - try to state them clearly, and to justify them if you can.

601 Mary was alone in the house when she went to bed and when she is alone she always leaves the hall light on, so it should still have been on when Dave got home. But he swears it was off. That means somebody else must have turned it off.

602 It is a good idea to signal your intentions well before you turn. In the first place you are more likely to find out what other drivers are going to do because they will follow your example. But more importantly, if you develop this habit you will learn to make up your mind earlier, and that will make you a better driver, as you will be less likely to act impulsively.

603 There is little point in saving money any more. If you are trying to survive on an ordinary salary - and few of us have any other resources - by the time you have paid your rent and bills there is very little left, so that it would take you years and years to save up even for a car, let alone a house. And with inflation, by that time what you have saved will be worth next to nothing.

604 One of the advantages of a folding kayak is that you can handle it entirely on your own. Then there is the sheer simplicity of it - just a few sticks and some canvas, plus a paddle. More practically Susan, your back is past its best, so you want a really light boat. All this means that you would find a folding kayak much more relaxing than some big heavy motorboat. And it would suit me better too - there would be enough money left over for that trip to Switzerland. So that's what you should get - an old fashioned folding kayak, not a smelly motorboat.

605 The engine is starting to give off a lot of smoke, and so it cannot be going to last much longer. This means we are not going to make it back home in the car. What is more, the leak in the radiator is getting worse, so the engine will overheat badly, especially on hills, and remember it is uphill most of the way home. So again, the car is not going to get us back. Clearly then, if we want to get home at all we will have to leave the car behind and go by bus, so we should book our seats right now.

606 If you buy an ice cream then Jenny will want to have one too, and you know she is not allowed to eat anything with sugar in it - the doctor says she has diabetes. The trouble is she does not realise how serious it is and there will be a terrible fuss if she sees you with something she is not allowed to have.

607 Many species of wetlands birdlife face extinction. With the spread of agriculture and increased urbanisation both their habitat and their very lives are threatened. Swamps are drained for new pasture land and agricultural pesticides kill off the insects upon which many birds depend, directly or indirectly. Moreover, since wetland birds tend to be poor fliers and nest at ground level, they are easy prey for domestic cats, and so with every new suburb, vast numbers are killed off.

608 Do not wear your high-heeled shoes to the circus, Anna. Remember that time you twisted your ankle and could not walk for three days. They have those same dangerous walkways at the circus. And if you snap off a heel you will have nothing to wear on Saturday night. Anyway it would look ridiculous - everyone else will be dressed casually.

609 I have never been able to understand why anyone buys a brand-new car. As I figure it out, they just are not worth the extra cost. A two-year-old car costs on the average no more than half the price of a new model. And major trouble is most unlikely in the first five years. That means you should get three good years' running for half the price of five. And there is this: about one car in twenty gives a lot of trouble right from the start. By the time it is two years old all that should have been sorted out for you.

610 Look, Tony, if you plant a tree so close to the house there will be all sorts of trouble in the next few years. The main drains are just a few metres away and the roots will get in and block them. That is very expensive to get fixed. Then you have to think about the leaves: if it is an evergreen it will shade the living room in winter, and that will not be very popular with Susan, and if it is deciduous the fallen leaves will block the gutters and mess up the yard.

611 Mother is upset, Harry - you have made another of those ugly water stains on the table. How many times do I have to tell you to use a saucer when you have a cup of coffee? It is very expensive getting the furniture repolished and we just cannot afford to do it again. It looks terrible too - imagine what people must think when they see ugly stains everywhere. And what an awful example you are setting to your little sister. I think that upsets Mother as much as the damage done to the furniture.

612 When you get back from your trip to Korea I want you to give an illustrated talk to the Travel Club. They have never had anything about Korea. So what say you use transparency film rather than colour print film in your camera? That way you can put together a show where everyone can see what you are talking about. And if they are any good you should be able to sell them to an agent or publisher - they much prefer transparencies as they give much better quality reproductions.

613 It is an absolute disgrace the way grown men are appearing in public in short trousers. There should be a law banning them anywhere except the beach. Why should we have to look at ugly hairy knees in the streets and the shops? It is an aesthetic assault, and we are entitled to protection. Think of the example they set for the young! No wonder they take drugs and dye their hair if their elders and betters do not bother to dress properly! If these men want to complain that long trousers are uncomfortably hot, all I can say is that they were good enough for better men than they - a little discomfort is good for the character!

614 We really should help Aunt Jean tidy up her garden this weekend. It has become such a mess that the neighbours are complaining it spoils the street, and we do not want to upset that Mr Jones over the road - after all he is our bank manager. And remember, she is fairly well off. Who knows, she may leave some of it to us, and then we will be able to pay off the mortgage and so you can get that new car. Anyway, even if she gives it all to a cats' home, we still should give her a hand - after all she is your poor mother's only sister.

615 All civilised countries have banned corporal punishment in schools. It is high time we followed suit. The practice is thoroughly discredited as damaging for students and teachers alike: bad for teachers because it encourages them to become tyrannical and sadistic, and a good teacher must be exactly the opposite; bad for the pupils because it is degrading. Unless they are treated like adults rather than performing animals they will never learn to conduct themselves with maturity and dignity. The other problem with corporal punishment is that it does not work. Indeed, the worst trouble-makers amongst the pupils take advantage of it as a means of drawing further attention to themselves.

616 You really should turn off that radio, Tom. You must know that it annoys the old lady next door. She needs to rest in the afternoon and if she cannot get to sleep it upsets her digestion for days. Anyway you should be working not listening to the radio. Your exams start in three days and you know you have hardly done any work since the summer.

617 I vote we eat out tonight. There is nothing in the fridge so if we are going to cook our own we will have to go shopping, and the car is not going so that would mean carrying it all back home and I am far too tired for that. And listen, there is this new fish restaurant they are all talking about. Jan went there last week and had a whole fish done that spicy Szechwan way - your favourite.

618 You must be tired, what with the party last night and all that work in the garden today. Why not go to bed early? You need to be up at the crack of dawn tomorrow. Remember your flight to Sydney leaves at nine in the morning and you want to be in good shape when you get there, or you will have no chance of getting the job.

619 David is simply hopeless at playing the violin. His wrist is not supple enough and his fingers are too short, so he cannot reach the strings properly, and anyway his ear is not anywhere near good enough to play it in tune. So he should give up the violin and switch to the flute. That would be easier to live with. Nobody can make a really horrible noise on a flute, not even David. And we would not have to buy him a new instrument. Remember that his violin is in very poor condition, but he could use Mary's flute which is as good as new.

620 *Find your own passage to assess.* The final test is to try your hand at really long passages of text. That is, at full chapters of books, or long newspaper or magazine articles. Of course you will have to summarise, as it will no longer be possible to mark the passage directly. In fact though, this is often quite easy. Anyway, that is the final exercise in this chapter - find some suitable chapter or article and give it the full treatment: Summary (including clarification), Structure diagram, Test the inferences for reliability. (And this time you may also try to work out whether the reasons are true - that is test for soundness, not only for validity - but please leave that until last.)

EXERCISE SIX - MODEL ANSWERS

Exercise 601

1/Mary was alone in the house when she went to bed/ and 2/when she is alone she always leaves the hall light on/, <so> 3/it should still have been on when Dave got home/. But 4/he swears it was off/. <That means> 5/somebody else must have turned it off/.

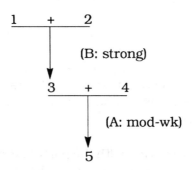

It is clearly a good idea to assess A before B: if A turns out to be weak then no amount of support through B is going to help the main conclusion, 5.

Inference A assumes that Dave is not mistaken, or lying. Stated generally, the unstated reason is:

When somebody swears that p, then p

where p is anything that somebody might swear. Now of course this is not always true, but (hopefully) it is considerably more likely to be true than false - that is, it is probable, and so the inference is moderately reliable. (If you are more sceptical, you may have ranked the inference as weak, on the ground that the unstated reason is improbable.)

Inference B is an interesting one. Start by looking closely at the conclusion - statement 3. What does it mean? The phrase "should be" suggests this reading:

> So long as nobody touched the switch in the meantime, the light would still have been on when Dave got home.

If that is how we interpret 3, then inference B is valid, and hence strong.

Exercise 602

1/It is a good idea to signal your intentions well before you turn/. <In the first place> 2/you are more likely to find out what other drivers are going to do/ <because> 3/they will follow your example/. But more importantly, 4/if you develop this habit you will learn to make up your mind earlier/, and 5/that will make you a better driver/, <as> 6/you will be less likely to act impulsively/.

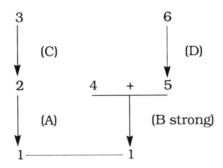

In this passage it is stated that B is more important than A. I think that this entitles us to concentrate on B, and I shall take the extreme step of ignoring A entirely. (Remember that this is a convergent argument and so if either main inference is all right then the conclusion is well supported.)

How good is B then? Are there any interesting counterexamples? Yes there are some. If you have good reason for misleading someone as to your intended route - say in one of those high-speed chases on TV - it could still be true that developing the habit of signalling early will make you a better driver but that it is not (on this occasion) a good idea to signal at all, or at least to signal correctly.

Of course for most of us these circumstances are most unlikely, and so while there are counterexamples, the inference is still a strong enough one.

If it had not turned out this way we should have had to turn to the other line of inference. As it is, though, the inference which is said in the passage to be the more important is a good enough one, so the other may be ignored.

Exercise 603

> 1/There is little point in saving money any more/. 2/If you are trying to survive on an ordinary salary/ - and 3/few of us have any other resources/ - 2[contd]/by the time you have paid your rent and bills there is very little left/, <so that> 4/it would take you years and years to save up even for a car, let alone a house/. And 5/with inflation, by that time what you have saved will be worth next to nothing/.

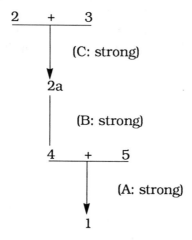

Remember that in number 325 (Exercise Three) I rewrote some of the reasons:

> 2a. By the time you have paid your rent and bills there is very little left.
> 3. You are trying to survive on an ordinary salary.

Looking first at A: can 4 and 5 be true while 1 is false?   There can be counterexamples to the inference - for example, if you are saving up for a packet of chewing gum rather than a yacht or a holiday on the Riviera - but they are trivial. If 4 and 5 are true, then it is hard to see how there could be any point in what we might call serious saving.

But wait. We must remember that "there is little point in" is rather an ambiguous expression. Sure, from my point of view there may be little point in saving if 4 and 5 are true, but from the point of view of the Reserve Bank or the Minister of Finance there may still be considerable point. Indeed it could perhaps be the best way for them to make 5 false. (At least I think this is what some of the economists sometimes try to tell us.)

So we should decide what 1 does mean. And surely in this passage it means from the point of view of the saver, not from the point of view of any large institution. In that case the "counterexample" is not a counterexample and the inference is strong.

Now we should look at the rest of the chain. Briefly, it looks good. If you have little left after your bills have been paid you will not be able to save quickly, so B is also strong. And if our interpretation of 3 is correct, C is a deductively valid inference.

Exercise 604

1/One of the advantages of a folding kayak is that you can handle it entirely on your own/. Then 2/there is the sheer simplicity of it - just a few sticks and some canvas, plus a paddle/. 3/More practically Susan, your back is past its best/, <so> 4/you want a really light boat/. <All this means that> 5/you would find a folding kayak much more relaxing than some big heavy motorboat/. And 6/it would suit me better too/ - 7/there would be enough money left over for that trip to Switzerland/<So> 8/that's what you should get - an old fashioned folding kayak, not a smelly motorboat/.

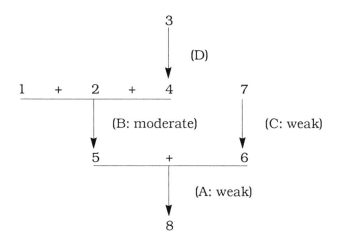

This may sound convincing, but do not let your romantic dreams carry you away. Inference A is a poor one. Counterexample: you want a boat for deep sea towing - this is consistent with 5 and 6 being true and 8 false.

Of course this sort of counterexample could easily be ruled out by changing the wording of the passage, but our job is to assess inferences as stated, not as intended. (Of course in the process we do hope to get much better at stating just what we intend to state.)

Inference C likewise is no good as stated. I may want a seagoing tug more than I want a trip to Switzerland, so there is a counterexample. Inference B is the best of them all. Of course you need to say that folding kayaks are light, but that apart it fares quite well. And indeed if we trouble also to say what Susan wants a boat for, this inference and the other ones become quite good. Unless she does want a seagoing tug!

Exercise 605

1/The engine is starting to give off a lot of smoke/, <and so> 2/it cannot be going to last much longer/. <This means> 3/we are not going to make it back home in the car/. What is more, 4/the leak in the radiator is getting worse/, <so> 5/the engine will overheat badly, especially on hills/, and remember 6/it is uphill most of the way home/. <So> again, 3/the car is not going to get us back/. <Clearly then>, 7/if we want to get home at all we will have to leave the car behind and go by bus/<so> 8/<u>we should book our seats right now</u>/.

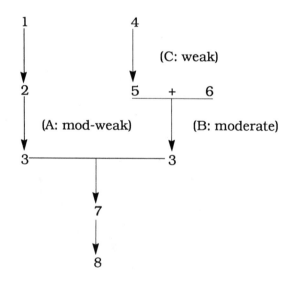

Usually it is wise to pick the last inference in an argument as the most important one, but here we should start with A and/or B. That is, the crucial question is whether the car is going to get us back home, not whether we have to book on the bus. Granted, if we have to book it may be an urgent matter, but that is not stated in the passage, and so I shall look at the reasons for 3.

Neither of the inferences is at all strong. In the case of A, the engine is not going to last much longer but it could well last long enough to get us back home. It is assumed that the engine has to last considerably longer if we are to get back home - that is, that the drive home is a long one. This is perhaps probable, perhaps improbable - the inference is moderate to weak.

And as for B, the unstated reason is that if the engine overheats badly we will not get back home. This is probable - engines have been known to survive severe overheating, granted, but it is not probable that they will. The inference is moderately reliable.

Finally, though, inference C is a weak one - the reason can be true with the conclusion false if we regularly fill the radiator.

Exercise 606

1/If you buy an ice cream then Jenny will want to have one too/, and you know 2/she is not allowed to eat anything with sugar in it/ - 3/the doctor says she has diabetes/. The trouble is 4/she does not realise how serious it is/ and 5/there will be a terrible fuss if she sees you with something she is not allowed to have/.

Unstated conclusion 6: <u>Do not buy an ice cream.</u>

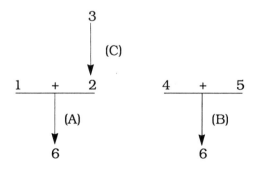

I suppose there is an unstated intermediate conclusion too, that it would be unfair to have one when Jenny is not allowed one. But that may not be how A is supposed to work - the idea might be that she will have one if we do and that will be bad for her. Indeed when we start trying to work out the logic of

A we see that what looks a straightforward piece of argumentation is really only the bones of an argument, and that it is the bones of more than one possible argument at that.

And rereading the passage I am no longer so sure that there are two independent lines of reasoning down to 6. Not that I blame myself for this - it is the passage that is to blame, not me. (I am trying to set you a certain example here!) But we must press on and do what we can, which is to find a counterexample: We all gobble lots and lots of ice cream but make sure that poor Jenny does not find out about it. Both lines of inference work on the assumption that she knows what is going on. A single counterexample is fatal to the whole structure.

This should be an object lesson. Often when we get ourselves into "structural" messes there is a short sharp way out. In this case, even without marking the passage and drawing an arrow diagram, it is obvious once it is pointed out that if we can keep Jenny in the dark all of the troubles mentioned can be avoided. You will find more and more as you work your way through this book that the various techniques you learn can often be abandoned, in many cases. You must develop the self-confidence to do without the formal apparatus, to explain the deficiencies of an argument in plain terms, accurately of course but without any technical props.

Exercise 607

> 1/Many species of wetlands birdlife face extinction/. 2/With the spread of agriculture and increased urbanisation both their habitat and their very lives are threatened/. 3/Swamps are drained for new pasture land/ and 4/agricultural pesticides kill off the insects upon which many birds depend, directly or indirectly/. Moreover, <since> 5/wetland birds tend to be poor fliers and nest at ground level/, 6/they are easy prey for domestic cats/, <and so> 7/with every new suburb, vast numbers are killed off/.

There are two rather different ways to diagram this. The one on the right has reason 2 split up:

2a. With the spread of agriculture and increased urbanisation, their habitat is threatened.

2b. With the spread of agriculture and increased urbanisation, their lives are threatened.

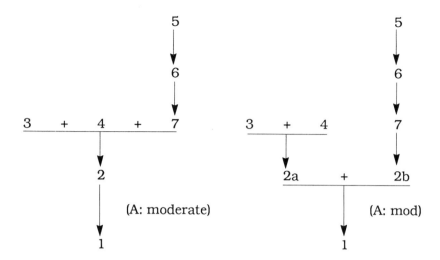

The right-hand diagram is the better of the two. If the argument that the habitat is threatened turns out to be weak, the argument that their lives are threatened might still be strong enough to warrant our accepting the conclusion. And vice versa. And in the passage, the two arguments are separated; 3 and 4 before "moreover", and 5 to 7 after it, which suggests that they are being treated as separate and independent issues.

It is easy in a case like this to get down to detail rather too soon. We should sit back and ask, even if 2a and 2b are both true, does that force us (on pain of contradiction) to accept the conclusion, to accept 1? To admit that a thing is under threat is not to admit that it faces any great peril. This could be a threat we know how to cope with. I am not saying that it is, but the argument does not rule this out, and to be valid it must do so.

Thus the key move, inference A, is as it stands no better than a moderately reliable one - it is not wildly improbable that we have arranged another home for these threatened species, well away from the dangers mentioned in the passage. Sure, it is not wildly probable either, so the inference is not a strong one.

It would be a mistake, though, to dismiss the argument on the ground that its main inference is only moderately reliable. Sometimes we are concerned to find out if there is any chance at all that something dreadful will happen. In these cases we may have to listen carefully even to inferences which are no better than weak. If the cost of an outcome is very high, then it may be well worth while to take steps to avoid even a remote possibility of that outcome. Many environmentalists argue that way about species, and most of us argue that way about health - our own if not everyone else's.

Exercise 608

1/Do not wear your high-heeled shoes to the circus, Anna/. Remember that time 2/you twisted your ankle and could not walk for three days 3/They have those same dangerous walkways at the circus/. And 4/if you snap off a heel you will have nothing to wear on Saturday night/<Anyway> 5/it would look ridiculous/ - 6/everyone else will be dressed casually/.

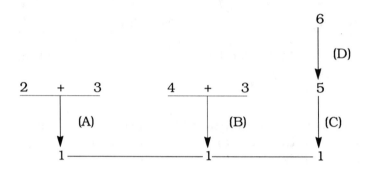

This one is not really as complex as it looks. Basically we have three more or less independent reasons for one conclusion.

And there are counterexamples: Anna has learned how to walk on those dangerous walkways without twisting her ankle; She does not care about Saturday night; She does not mind looking ridiculous. So even if we replace A to C with a single inference arrow and put in plus signs between 3 and 4 and 5, the inference still would not be valid.

That is about all one can say. This is about Anna, and we do not know her. In particular we do not know exactly how likely it is that she does not mind looking ridiculous, and that is precisely what we have to know to arrive at any more definite grading of the inferences.

Exercise 609

1/I have never been able to understand why anyone buys a brand-new car/. As I figure it out, 2/they just are not worth the extra cost/. 3/ A two-year-old car costs on the average no more than half the price of a new model/. And 4/major trouble is most unlikely in the first five years/. <That means> 5/you should get three good years' running for half the price of five/. And there is this: 6/about one car in twenty gives a lot of trouble right from the start/. 7/By the time it is two years old all that should have been sorted out for you/.

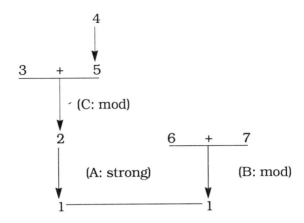

I have marked the first sentence as the final conclusion, but it needs to be restated:

1. It is much better not to buy a brand-new car.

Looking at B first: this will not convince someone who hates to be seen in an old car, who is prepared to put up with all manner of teething troubles to sit behind the wheel of the latest model. Likely trouble on its own is scarcely a reason one way or another. That is, B assumes that a rather small chance of major trouble is a compelling reason for avoiding something. While it would be irrational to ignore this sort of consideration, it does not outweigh all others. For this reason, I rank B as moderate.

Inference A is strong - by that stage it is already conceded that new cars are not worth the extra cost. That is, it is conceded that they have no advantages which outweigh the cost disadvantage. And that is what is assumed by step C. Perhaps only a few of us can ignore the costs, but is it true that some people are in a position to do this, and there are some who are not but who act as if they are. So again, I rate the inference as moderate. It is probable but not highly probable that there are no advantages which outweigh the economic disadvantage.

Exercise 610

Look, Tony, 1/if you plant a tree so close to the house there will be all sorts of trouble in the next few years/. 2/The main drains are just a few metres away/ and <so> 3/the roots will get in and block them/. 4/ That is very expensive to get fixed/. Then you have to think about the leaves: 5/if it is an evergreen it will shade the living room in winter/ and 6/that will not be very popular with Susan/, and 7/if it is deciduous the fallen leaves will block the gutters and mess up the yard/.

Unstated conclusion 8: <u>Do not plant a tree so close to the house.</u>

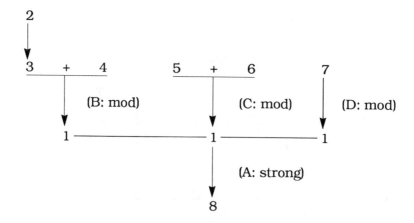

We all know how to do the easy counterexample to A, I trust? If what we are looking for is all manner of trouble then 1 can be true without being anything like a reason for not planting a tree close to the house. On the contrary, that is exactly what we are looking for. Of course, this easy counterexample is a most unlikely one, and the inference is strong.

The other job is to look at the support for 1. If we grant that this applies to normal idle people who do not indulge in unnecessary exertion let alone seek out trouble, then all of these look like fairly good reasons - provided there is nothing else at stake. But we may want a lot of summer shade, and be prepared to put up with fallen leaves and blocked drains in order to get this, or we may want to attract a lot of birds, or we may just love trees. So again there are lots of counterexamples, and again they will have differing likelihoods with different people.

Exercise 611

1/Mother is upset/, Harry - 2/you have made another of those ugly water stains on the table/. How many times do I have to tell you to 3/<u>use a saucer when you have a cup of coffee/</u>? 4/It is very expensive getting the furniture repolished/ and 5/we just cannot afford to do it again/. 6/It looks terrible too/ - imagine 7/what people must think when they see ugly stains everywhere/. And 8/what an awful example you are setting to your little sister/! I think that upsets Mother as much as the damage done to the furniture.

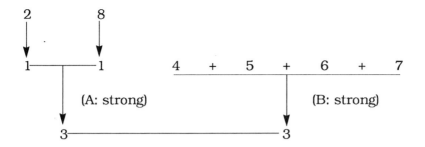

Strictly, 7 should be reworded: People will be upset when they see the stains.

Of course we must not upset Mother! A difficulty in dealing with this sort of example is that it uses a sort of unstated "rule" - don't upset Mother - which is hard to reject but of course ridiculous to accept. I do not mean that it is perfectly all right to make her life a misery, but on the other hand it would be plain stupid (if not wicked) to elevate this into a rule which overrides all other rules. So if the only way to obtain some other great good (say studying logic rather than accountancy) involves (probably) upsetting Mother (who knows what is best), we should at least consider upsetting her.

But as long as using a saucer is a relatively simple matter we do not have to solve these deep mysteries of Moral Philosophy. We can accept that if all we have to do to avoid upsetting the Old Thing is to remember to use a saucer then almost certainly one should use a saucer. That is exactly what inference A assumes, so it is strong.

Again in the case of B, as long as it is no great trouble to use a saucer, the reasons are fairly compelling. Together they block the most likely counterexamples: 6 says that the stains look terrible, so we cannot consider the possibility that we don't care about them. We may not care what other people think, though, but that is highly unlikely when "we" think the stains look terrible. So B is strong also.

Exercise 612

1/When you get back from your trip to Korea I want you to give an illustrated talk to the Travel Club/. 2/They have never had anything about Korea/. So what say you 3/use transparency film rather than colour print film in your camera/? <That way> 4/you can put together a show where everyone can see what you are talking about/. And 5/ if they are any good you should be able to sell them to an agent or publisher/ - 6/they much prefer transparencies/ <as> 7/they give much better quality reproductions/.

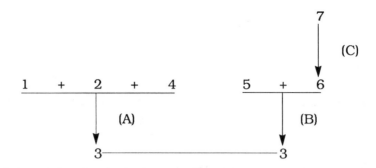

Like so many of our examples, it is all too easy to drift along with the flow of the argument without realising that there may be good and even pressing reasons for doing exactly the opposite. And here of course there might be all sorts of reasons for using colour print film rather than transparencies, all consistent with the reasons.

There is more than one way of making the point. One would be more or less to grant what is argued in the passage, but then go on to argue the case for colour prints: one's hatred of giving illustrated talks, especially to Travel Clubs, one's total lack of interest in publication, one's personal preference for prints in albums, the cost perhaps, and so on.

A rather different looking way of achieving much the same end is to use some of these same moves in constructing counterexamples rather than counterarguments. So for example, the ability to put on a public performance (reason 4) does not yield the conclusion that you should use transparencies (conclusion 3) if (counterexample) you do not want to be able to put on a public performance.

Exercise 613

> 1/It is an absolute disgrace the way grown men are appearing in public in short trousers/. 2/There should be a law banning them anywhere except the beach/. Why should we have to look at ugly hairy knees in the streets and the shops? 3/It is an aesthetic assault/, and 4/we are entitled to protection/. Think of 5/the example they set to the young/! No wonder 6/they take drugs and dye their hair/ if 5/ their elders and betters do not bother to dress properly/! If these men want to complain that long trousers are uncomfortably hot, all I can say is that 7/they were good enough for better men than they/ - 8/a little discomfort is good for the character/!

Rewriting 5: Grownup men wearing shorts set a bad example to the young.

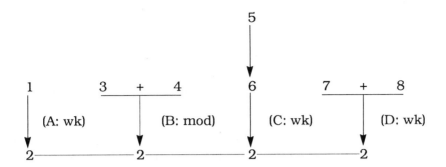

Inferences like A are common in the letters to the editor of the local newspaper. The unstated reason is that anything which is absolutely disgraceful should be outlawed. But we would want to be persuaded for example that making something illegal would actually reduce its incidence rather than increase it. And we might also want to be convinced that the "absolutely disgraceful" conduct is actually harmful. Hence, the unstated reason is improbable - the inference is weak.

The aesthetic argument, B, assumes that the only way to prevent the "aesthetic assault" is to ban short trousers. This is not so. One alternative would be to ridicule them, so that nobody will dare appear in public in them. Another is to change the aesthetic responses of those who dislike them, so that they come to appreciate short trousers. Of course neither of these would be at all easy in practice; it is probably true, accepting the other reasons as true, that banning shorts is the best way to protect the fastidious, and so we could grade this as a moderately reliable inference. Remember that we are assessing reliability, not soundness - so we are accepting statements 3 and 4, at present.

Inferences like C and D also tend to appear in the letters page of the local newspaper. C assumes that it is because of this baleful influence that the young misbehave. That is so improbable that the inference is weak. And D is no better. The unstated reason here is that development of character is a sufficient condition for passing a law.

Important new technique

A comment here on applying the probability test for reliability of unstated reasons. In cases like this one it is rather awkward to apply the idea of probability. When you find that this is the case, I suggest that you replace the test question with one in terms of *acceptability*:

The reliability of an inference is

Strong	-	When the unstated reasons are *highly acceptable.*
Moderate	-	When the unstated reasons are *acceptable.*
Weak	-	When the unstated reasons are *unacceptable.*

Indeed, this concept of acceptability could replace that of probability in all of our definitions and tests. After all, a reason which is probably not true is unacceptable, one whose truth is probable is acceptable, and one whose truth is highly probable is highly acceptable.

So, if you are unhappy using the concept of probability in any example, try this concept of acceptability. It is particularly useful where the reasons involve ethical claims and the like, where it is not obviously the case that they can be called true or false, but where we have little trouble deciding which ones we regard as acceptable and which as unacceptable.

Returning now to D: The statement that the development of character is a sufficient condition for passing a law which restricts our behaviour is unacceptable. For two reasons: First, because such laws have little chance of success, and second, because character - as opposed to one's behaviour - is basically one's own business.

A final comment. Alternative structure diagrams yield importantly different inferences, here as elsewhere. In particular, the question whether the main inferences are in support of 2 - as in my diagram - or 1 - as in a plausible alternative - is not settled by the wording of the passage.

Exercise 614

1/We really should help Aunt Jean tidy up her garden this weekend/ 2/It has become such a mess that the neighbours are complaining it spoils the street/, and 3/we do not want to upset that Mr Jones over the road/ - <after all> 4/he is our bank manager/. And remember, 5/she is fairly well off/. Who knows, 6/she may leave some of it to us/ <and then> 7/we will be able to pay off the mortgage/ <and so> 8/you can get that new car/. Anyway, even if she gives it all to a cats' home, 1/we still should give her a hand/ - <after all> 9/she is your poor mother's only sister/.

Unstated intermediate conclusion 10: It is to our advantage to help her.

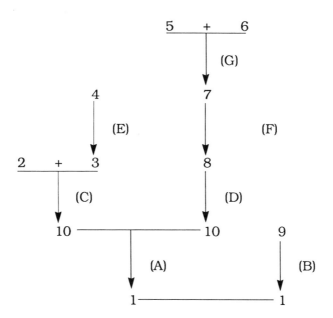

I am using the second of the two diagrams from Chapter Three, because it separates the two very different types of consideration used here - the moral argument of inference B and the prudential argument of inference A.

To assess B at all thoroughly would take us deep into Moral Philosophy, so I shall turn to A. But wait - in turning to A we cannot just ignore inferences like B, because this is just the type of inference we are likely to come up with as counterexamples to A. Consider this scenario: All of the reasons supporting 10 are true, as is 10, but it is also the case that Aunt Jean has acted unforgivably towards her sister. On these grounds we reject 1. That is, we have true reasons and a false conclusion, and we got them by adding an accepted-as-true reason of a very different sort - more like 9 than the others.

The crucial point in all this is to see that A is a weak inference. For example, we may be altruists, in which case we are quite likely to act against our own best interests. So A is not at all reliable.

Then there is the question whether 10 is true. Is it? Consider these possibilities: Mr Jones likes untidy gardens; Mr Jones does not know that Aunt Jean is related to us in any way; Mr Jones cannot use his position to our disadvantage; Mr Jones would not stoop to using his position to our disadvantage. In all of these cases, and the others that have occurred to you, the reason for 10 can be true while 10 is false. And they are distinct possibilities. So 10 is not well supported.

Overall this is not an easy argument to assess, as the prudential and moral considerations are hard to weigh up against each other. But in brief I would say (a) that 10 is not well supported, and (b) that even if it is true the conclusion does not follow, from 10 or from 9.

Exercise 615

1/All civilised countries have banned corporal punishment in schools/ 2/It is high time we followed suit/. 3/The practice is thoroughly discredited/ as damaging for students and teachers alike: 4/bad for teachers/ <because> 5/it encourages them to become tyrannical and sadistic/and 6/a good teacher must be exactly the opposite/; 7/bad for the pupils/ <because> 8/it is degrading. Unless they are treated like adults rather than performing animals/ 9/they will never learn to conduct themselves with maturity and dignity/. The other problem with corporal punishment is that 10/it does not work/. <Indeed>, 11/ the worst trouble-makers amongst the pupils take advantage of it as a means of drawing further attention to themselves/.

Rewriting some of the statements:
3. Corporal punishment is thoroughly discredited.
4. Corporal punishment is bad for teachers.
7. Corporal punishment is bad for pupils.
8. With corporal punishment pupils are treated like performing animals rather than adults.
9. If pupils are not treated like adults they will never learn to conduct themselves with maturity and dignity.

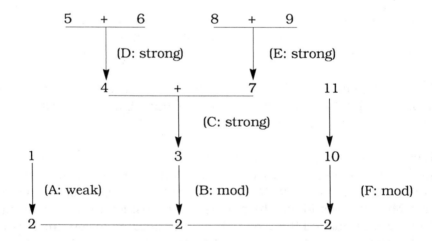

I commented on this example in number 337 (Chapter Three) that we have almost reached the stage where marking the reasons and conclusions directly on the text is a waste of time, and suggested that the thing to do is write out all of the reasons and conclusions in your own words.

And we have approached the stage where a single diagram is hardly any use to us, and here I suggest that smaller diagrams which depict only some of the stated relations may be all that we need.

Of course the full diagram is not at all difficult to construct, but it has no particular advantage over the corresponding three diagrams, involving respectively inferences A, B and F:

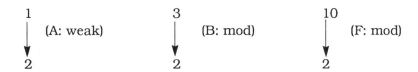

The argument from 1 to 2 is easily disposed of. Some people are of the opinion that every civilised country lies to the north of the Equator, but this does not commit them to the view that moving Australia into the North Atlantic would even change its climate let alone turn it into a civilised place. It is strange how persistent some of the fallacious patterns of reasoning are. Here we need to know not that civilised countries have this feature but that they need it. Or you might put it this way: we are told that all civilised countries do have this feature when what we need (if we are to make the inference validly) is that any country with this feature is civilised. That, though, is improbable, and so the inference is weak.

Turning to B, if teachers and students are the only parties involved then B is all right. But are they? Can we be sure that others would not be harmed if the practice were abandoned? No, not quite. But we can be reasonably sure, and so the inference is moderately reliable, at least.

Inference C is deductively valid.

The real meat of the argument is in inferences D and E:

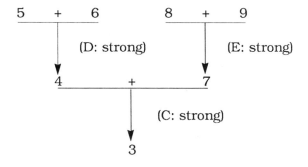

As it is worded, D is not easy to fault. But it is not quite faultless - it assumes that something that produces bad teachers will be bad for teachers. But that is highly probable, and so the inference is strong. Likewise, E is strong: something that degrades you is thereby bad for you.

The trouble with the other "flanking" argument is that it does not say what corporal punishment is supposed to do. I think that it is being assumed that it is meant to act as a deterrent. And that is at least probable, so the inference is at least moderately reliable.

Exercise 616

1/You really should turn off that radio, Tom/. You must know that 2/ it annoys the old lady next door/. 3/She needs to rest in the afternoon/ and 4/if she cannot get to sleep it upsets her digestion for days/. Anyway 5/you should be working not listening to the radio/. 6/Your exams start in three days/ and you know 7/you have hardly done any work since the summer/.

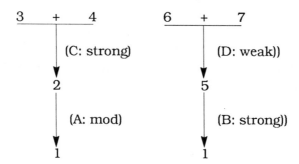

Counterexamples to inference A: The old lady next door is meant to get up and go to work but she is lazy and stays in bed unless she is annoyed by something like Tom's radio. Of course this is scarcely compatible with 3 and 4, and anyway it is rather unlikely. As I think are any other counterexamples. And if that is so then A is a moderately good inference.

Inference B is hard to fault, which is not surprising given the wording of 5. But D is not a good inference: Tom may be so brilliant that he does not need to do any work, or he may have good reasons for wanting to fail. Or there may be something coming up on the radio that he needs to know for his exams, or for some other good reason.

Exercise 617

I vote 1/we eat out tonight/. 2/There is nothing in the fridge/ <so> 3/if we are going to cook our own we will have to go shopping/, and 4/the car is not going/ <so> 5/that would mean carrying it all back home/ and 6/I am far too tired for that/. And listen, 7/there is this new fish restaurant they are all talking about/. 8/Jan went there last week and had a whole fish done that spicy Szechwan way/ - 9/your favourite/.

Rewriting:

1. Let us eat out tonight
8. The new restaurant serves spicy Szechwan whole fish
9. That is your favourite.

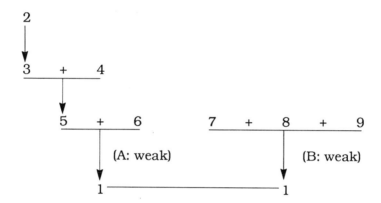

Inference A involves, basically, deciding to eat out because we do not want to cook our own meal. The unstated reason is that whenever people do not want to cook, they can eat out. That is improbable. In a great number of cases - surely the vast majority - eating out is not a real option. There will be nowhere suitable to go, where "suitable" includes suitably inexpensive. Thus, inference A is weak.

Inference B is weak too, and for much the same reason. The availability even of one's favourite dish is not enough, on its own. Again it is assumed that one can afford to eat out, and this is very often not the case.

In drawing your diagram you may have linked the reasons up more than I have, like this:

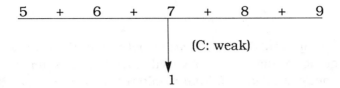

I have drawn it the other way because the last three reasons sound as if they are meant to be taken independently of the others. But the alternative reading is reasonable, too. And although we might expect C to come out stronger than A or B, in fact it too is a weak inference, and for the same reason. Even this combination of reasons assumes that we can afford to eat out, and that is as improbable as ever.

Exercise 618

1/You must be tired/, <what with> 2/the party last night/ and 3/all that work in the garden today/. Why not 4/<u>go to bed early</u>/? 5/You need to be up at the crack of dawn tomorrow/. Remember 6/your flight to Sydney leaves at nine in the morning/ and 7/you want to be in good shape when you get there/, or 8/you will have no chance of getting the job/.

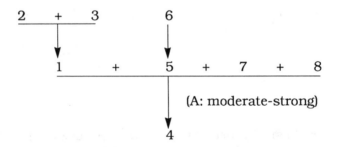

Note that several statements need rewriting. E.g. 2: You went to the party last night. Etc.

In number 336 (Chapter 3) I diagrammed this as a convergent argument. On reflection, it seems better to represent it as linked. In particular, if you were not tired, the other reasons would not start to be reasons, and so 1 is not in-dependant of the others.

Inference A: Counterexample when there is a good reason for staying up despite the tiredness - e.g. you want to do more exercises from this book. It is unlikely though that this would outweigh the others, so inference A is moderately reliable, perhaps even strong.

Exercise 619

1/David is simply hopeless at playing the violin/ - 2/his wrist is not supple enough/ and 3/his fingers are too short/, <so> 4/he cannot reach the strings properly/, and anyway 5/his ear is not anywhere near good enough to play it in tune/. <So> 6/he should give up the violin and switch to the flute/. 7/That would be easier to live with/. 8/Nobody can make a really horrible noise on a flute, not even David/ And 9/we would not have to buy him a new instrument/. Remember that 10/his violin is in very poor condition/, but 11/he could use Mary's flute/ 12/which is as good as new/.

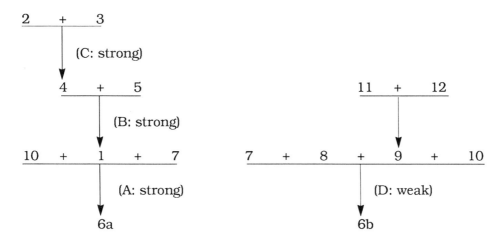

There are several possible structure diagrams for this passage. After a few false starts, I have settled upon this pair of diagrams, where the two final conclusions are:

6a. David should give up the violin.
6b. David should take up the flute.

I have put 7 and 10 in both arguments as they relate both to giving up the violin and to taking up the flute.

My false starts all involved trying to fit the whole passage into a single diagram. In the end I decided that there are two conclusions which are almost completely independent of each other. Hence the two independent diagrams.

The reason I am attending so carefully to structure at this stage is to remind you that questions of reliability and questions of logical structure are intimately connected. You must always be prepared to alter your diagrams. Often, what seems to be the structure on a first reading turns out to be quite inadequate when you get deep into an appraisal of the adequacy of the inferences. Whatever you do, do not just stick to the original diagram "come what may". Throw it away, start afresh.

Inference A assumes that people who are hopeless at the violin should give it up. That in turn assumes that they will get no better. But the other reasons in the passage more or less write off any chance of improvement, in David's case. And if it is true that he will not improve, then we can definitely accept that he should give up, given that he is hopeless. That is, A is strong. So are B and C. The case for giving up the violin in impressive.

The other argument is nowhere near as good. Inference D assumes that he should play some instrument. There is no really positive case for the flute. And remember, he does not have a good ear. The argument assumes that you do not need a good ear to play the flute, and this is false. So D is weak too.

Meaning and Inference   7

You will often have noticed how the reliability of an inference can depend upon the meanings of the words used.

This works in two ways. The meanings can help validate an inference, ranging from the merest suggestion of support for a conclusion to a completely valid inference based solely upon meanings. On the other hand, there are various ways in which meanings can invalidate an inference. Some of the most subtle and persistent fallacies are connected with the meanings of words. In this chapter we shall take time out to examine these relations between meaning and inference.

The first half of the chapter deals mostly with ways in which meanings can help validate an inference, and the second half concentrates upon fallacies.

To start with something clear-cut, here are two simple valid arguments:

A. Harry is an accountant, and accountants are mean, so he must be mean.
B. Jennifer is a widow, so she has been married.

One obvious difference between them is that A has two reasons while B has only one. In A, if we remove the second reason the argument is no longer valid. The link between *being an accountant* and *being mean* has to be stated.

But the link in B between *being a widow* and *having been married* does not have to be stated. Of course we could add to B the statement that all widows have been married, but the argument is already valid as it is, without the added reason. It is not something which could have been otherwise: To be a widow means, amongst other things, to have been married.

Contrast this with A: To be an accountant does not mean to be mean. This could be otherwise. (Indeed it is otherwise -- there are many accountants who do not fit the crude stereotype.) This is why the validity of the argument depends crucially on whether the argument contains the statement that all accountants are mean.

The matter can be put like this: Both A and B involve a universal statement - "All accountants are mean" and "All widows have been married". In the case of A the statement has to be made while in the case of B it does not. The reason for this is that the statement that all widows have been married is necessarily true. We are entitled to take it as true, in any argument. On the other hand, even if it were true that all accountants are mean, we would not be entitled to assume that it is true. If we want to use it we have to state it.

All of this is to illustrate the fact that the inferences we make can depend for their validity upon the meanings of words. In this case, "widow" and "married".

Of course it is not often quite as straightforward as this. Most of the relations between meanings that feature in our arguments are looser than the link between "widow" and "married".

For example, consider Dawn, who is a health faddist, eating beans rather than meat and drinking herb tea rather than coffee. When I say that she is a health faddist it does not follow that she eats beans rather than meat. But there is a connection. It is this: when we call someone a heath faddist we are already saying that they do that sort of thing. Not specifically that they eat beans and drink herb tea, but if it is not that it will be vitamins or jogging or kelp granules or vast amounts of fish. And we know how to continue the list.

I do not just mean that it is a matter of fact about health faddists that they do this sort of thing. No, what I mean is that if Dawn didn't do any of these things we would not be entitled to call her a health faddist. There is a connection in meaning, even if it is not simple and determinate like the one between "widowed" and "has been married".

When you think about it, many of the words we use are like this: when we use them we indicate - strongly or faintly - that some other word or words will be applicable.

You can see how this enters into the question of reliability. At one extreme we have examples like "widow": there the reason (she is a widow), if true, makes it absolutely certain that the conclusion is true (she has been married). There is a completely valid inference, based upon the meanings of words. Towards the other extreme we have Dawn: Here the reason (she is a health faddist) makes it rather more probable than usual that the conclusion is true (she eats beans and drinks herb tea). Here the inference based upon the meanings of the words is only a weak one.

One complication is that many of the words we use are *vague*, and many are *ambiguous*. In these cases, what inference if any is justified can depend upon exactly which sense of a word is used.

An *ambiguous* word, of course, is one which has more than one sense. Like "plant" - a botanical organism, or an industrial or manufacturing concern. These are entirely separate and distinct senses:

botanical organisms	industrial concerns

Both of those senses of "plant" are slightly vague. Is a beansprout a plant? When does it become one? There is no precise stage at which it suddenly becomes a plant. The borders between plants and non-plants are fuzzy:

Often, when we are analysing an argument, we will have to spell out exactly what sense of a word is appropriate. Of course there is in itself nothing wrong with using vague or ambiguous words. Indeed, there can be clear advantages in doing so. But on the other hand, we will frequently have to clarify the meanings of certain words in a passage, replacing them with more precise ones if we can. And we will sometimes come across straightforward fallacies, which result from the careless or dishonest use of vague or ambiguous words.

But before we attend to the fallacies, it is worthwhile to get in some practice with valid inferences which depend upon the meanings of words.

Exercises

Turn to Exercise Seven and work on numbers 701-723.

Fallacies

Many Logic books have a long section on fallacies, with a complex taxonomy using impressive Latin expressions like *argumentum ad verecundum* and *secundum quid.* This is typically followed by a list of passages which the reader is asked to classify, like botanical specimens.

Although that can be fun, the techniques you have already learned in this book are strong enough to work out what is wrong with almost any faulty inference. And that is just what a fallacy is - a faulty inference. So you do not need any taxonomy. Instead, I am presenting you with a set of exercises. Any impressive Latin names will emerge, as optional extras, in the Model Answers. But the important thing is to apply the basic principles to each case.

Exercises

Work on Exercise Seven numbers 724-750.

EXERCISE SEVEN

Questions 701-723: What follows?

Write down a statement which follows from the reason given.
Make sure that the statement follows from this reason alone.
The inference must be valid.
Make sure that it follows in virtue of the meanings of the words.
Explain. (Often it helps to point out what does not follow.)

701 There is no need to worry - Charles is a punctual fellow.

702 The river has a twisting convoluted course.

703 Robin is an Admiral.

704 Tony has been locked away in prison for the last five years.

705 The robber wore a mask.

706 Felix is a cat.

707 Jacob wears a yarmulka.

708 The glass is fragile.

709 Peter has a red nose.

710 Urea is a nitrate.

711 Everyone knows that two plus two equals four.

712 *Cedrus deodara* is a conifer.

713 The floor is made of marble.

714 Little Tommie is selfish.

715 Little Tommie is a liar.

716 That is an antique.

717 Poor Mary had a stroke.

718 Hamish plays the bagpipes.

719 Eric drives a pre-1930 car.

720 Mr Martin is a prudent fellow.

721 Janice promised to give it back.

722 The forecast is for fine weather.

723 Louis is saving up for a Stradavarius.

Questions 724-735: Do the meanings of the words used contribute to the strength of the inferences in these passages?
Comment on any logical weakness which are related to the meanings of the words.

724 The Volga river flows through Auckland and on through Mexico City to the sea. So Auckland must be higher than Mexico City.

725 Plato maintained that knowledge of the everyday mundane world is not true knowledge, as this world is a mere shadow or reflection of the true world, the World of Forms.

726 You cannot have that. It is mine.

727 Being unable to see, bats have to use a form of radar to avoid obstacles when flying.

728 It must have been John who ate that last piece of cake - he cannot resist it.

729 We give you the best deal in town because we guarantee to match any firm's regular price on any of our lines.

730 A private commercial college can offer courses for as little as $3500 per year and make a tidy profit. The real cost per course in the university system is three times this sum. The conclusion is obvious - our universities are inefficient and should be sold off into private ownership.

731 The occasional setback is good for us, because it reminds us that anything worth having is worth fighting for, and helps us to set clear goals.

732 Too much aspirin is bad for your digestion. When you have a headache you should take something else.

733 As all energy changes are at least to some extent irreversible, it follows that the entropy of the universe must be continuously increasing. Eventually it will attain its maximum, and then the universe will reach its heat death - no more energy will be available to do work.

734 This land was more or less empty when my ancestors arrived here. They took over only what they needed and developed it to serve those needs, clearing bush for their farms, building roads and bridges and towns and cities. It is ludicrous to suggest that it must all be returned to the previous inhabitants. It has become our property by virtue of the improvements made by generations of hard-working and God-fearing settlers.

735 It is a mistake to allow our schools to cater for what the pupils want. What matters is not what they want but what they need, and we adults must be the judges of that. More than ever, today's children need to master basic language and mathematical skills. The curriculum must concentrate upon these, however unpopular they may be.

Nos 736-750 - Fallacies: Decide precisely what, if anything, is wrong with the reasoning in each passage. Explain clearly.

You will find some technical fallacy-names in the model answers. Use these if you wish, in subsequent exercises, but make sure that you also explain in plain English what is wrong. That is the object of the exercise.

736 If we are going to provide free education for the young we should also provide it for anyone else who wants it.

737 There never has been any direct and positive proof that electrons actually exist. What we are shown are always the so-called effects of electrons, never the electrons themselves. Clearly, they are purely figments of the physicist's underemployed imagination.

738 Fascism cannot be anything like as bad as it is made out to be. Look how many ordinary sensible Germans joined the Nazis, and were prepared even to die, fighting for a Fascist society.

739 If you don't attend all of the classes and submit the essays on time you will fail. Anyone who is interested in the course will be prepared to do the work required, and if you aren't interested there is no way I can pass you.

740 There is nothing inherently wrong with warfare. Sure, it involves killing people, but when your life is threatened you are no longer required to respect the lives of others.

741 Tom Smith is a real bad egg. All of the trouble-makers end up as union officials, and he has just been elected secretary of the Drivers' Union.

742 No Western European nation could hope to mount a successful military attack on the USSR, so the Soviet Union has nothing serious to fear from Western Europe.

743 I wouldn't listen to what Harry says about repairing cars if I were you. Just look at his! It must be all of fifteen years old, and it's always giving him trouble. And everyone knows that he drinks far too much.

744 If you chop that tree down there will be another drought this summer. Didn't they teach you at school that trees increase the rainfall?

745 There was none of this gang violence and rape when I was young and people still went to Church!

746 You must agree that my answers are the correct ones. After all I am the examiner, and if you answer incorrectly I will be forced to fail you.

747 All of the top managers in the company wear grey suits and white shirts and black shoes, so if you want to get to the top you had better follow their example.

748 Freud's entire theory of human sexuality has been exposed as worthless, as no more than the drug-induced fantasy of a cocaine addict.

749 I never had a single day sick in bed until I moved here to Auckland. It must be a really unhealthy place.

750 Surely there must be some truth in astrology! Countless wise people have believed in it over the centuries, and have been prepared to entrust the entire running of their lives to the influences of the heavenly bodies.

EXERCISE SEVEN - MODEL ANSWERS

Exercise 701

> Reason: There is no need to worry - Charles is a punctual fellow.
> Conclusion: He is unlikely to be late.

It does not follow that he will not be late. Punctuality is a disposition, and we would not say that Charles is not punctual simply because he is very occasionally late.

Exercise 702

> Reason: The river has a twisting convoluted course.
> Conclusion: It is not straight.

It is also almost certain to be mature, to be passing through flat country and falling only slowly. But this does not follow strictly from the meanings of the words. That is a geological matter.

Exercise 703

> Reason: Robin is an Admiral.
> Conclusion: Robin is in the Navy.

It does not follow that Robin is male, as it would say if the reason were that

Robin is an uncle. If the Navy refuses to promote women to the rank of Admiral that is not because the meanings of the words preclude this.

Exercise 704

> Reason: Tony has been locked away in prison for the last five years.
> Conclusion: Tony has been in captivity.

But not that he has broken the law, or even that he has been accused of so doing. Of course we would hope that he will not be locked up unless he has broken the law, but the very fact that we can hope this shows that it is not logically impossible.

Exercise 705

> Reason: The robber wore a mask.
> Conclusion: Part of his or her face was covered.

It does not follow of course that the robber was unrecognisable.

Exercise 706

> Reason: Felix is a cat.
> Conclusion: Felix is a mammal.

In fact, "cat" is ambiguous: At the sailing club they would conclude that Felix is a two-hulled boat - a catamaran. That aside, note that in the more familiar sense of "cat" it does not follow that Felix has a tail or fur or says "meow". That is, if we were to meet something which lacked any one of these features we would not thereby be entitled to deny that it is a cat. Of course if it lacked all of them it might be a different matter - cf. my remarks about Dawn, the health-faddist.

Exercise 707

> Reason: Jacob wears a yarmulka.
> Conclusion: He wears a skullcap.

It does not follow though that he is Jewish. You may have had to use the dictionary, but take care. Mine defines it as a skullcap worn by Jewish men, but that means that it is typically worn by Jewish men, not that it would suddenly cease to be a yarmulka if an Eskimo woman were to try it on. Of course our statement that Jacob wears a yarmulka can be taken to mean, likewise, that he typically does this, not simply that he is doing so on a particular occasion. But even that does not show that he is Jewish.

Exercise 708

> Reason: The glass is fragile.
> Conclusion: It will break rather easily.

Fragility is a disposition: to say that the glass is fragile entails that if there are certain conditions then something will happen. Strictly the conclusion is: If it is struck firmly then it will break.

Exercise 709

> Reason: Peter has a red nose.
> Conclusion: Peter has a nose that is not green.

Or not purple, etc. Or even, that he has a nose. But not, of course, anything about the amount he drinks.

Exercise 710

> Reason: Urea is a nitrate.
> Conclusion: Urea contains oxygen - or that it contains nitrogen.

Note that I do not know whether urea is in fact a nitrate. And I do not even have to know what a nitrate is, let alone what urea is, to know that the conclusion follows. Both the dictionaries on my desk say that nitrates contain NO_3 - one says it directly and one via the definition of "nitric acid". And I remember enough chemistry to infer that there is nitrogen here, and oxygen.

Note also that for this we do not have to decide between the scientific definition of "urea" and the everyday one (the latter in terms of the source, the former in terms of the composition). All sorts of word could be substituted for "urea" in the reason and the suitably modified conclusion would follow.

The alert reader will notice that here I am treating a dictionary definition (of "nitrate") as logically binding, a move I have rejected elsewhere. Do not adopt the view that dictionary definitions are never strict enough for our purposes. Sometimes they are. The hard part is knowing when.

Exercise 711

> Reason: Everyone knows that two plus two equals four.
> Conclusion: I know that two plus two equals four.

And so do you. Many philosophers would also argue that it also follows that two plus two does indeed equal four - that one cannot properly be said to know that *p* unless it is also the case that *p*. But many philosophers argue many things: Here I will leave it with the philosophically unhelpful remark that if they are right then it also follows that two plus two does equal four.

Note that all of these remarks would still hold if we were to change "four" to "five" in the reason and the conclusion.

Exercise 712

> Reason: *Cedrus deodara* is a conifer.
> Conclusion: It is a plant.

If you are a botanist you may know some other defining characteristics of the conifers and will have come up with a more spectacular conclusion. But you do not have to be a botanist to know to be careful here. It does not for instance follow that it is a tree - some conifers are tiny shrubs. There is no need to comment on the ambiguity of "plant" in this sort of context - it is perfectly clear which sense is being used.

Exercise 713

> Reason: The floor is made of marble.
> Conclusion: The floor is made of stone.

The image comes to mind of highly polished stone, but this does not follow logically. If someone wants to make a floor of unfinished marble they may have made an architectural blunder but scarcely a semantic one.

Exercise 714

> Reason: Little Tommie is selfish.
> Conclusion: He cares too little for others.

It does not follow though that he does not care for them at all, even if he is very selfish.

Exercise 715

> Reason: Little Tommie is a liar.
> Conclusion: He often tells lies.

But not that he never tells the truth, even if he is an inveterate liar.

Exercise 716

Reason: That is an antique.
Conclusion: It is old.

What about: It is valuable? I do not think that quite follows. One of my dictionaries says an antique is "rare or valued" but the other one mentions age only. Note that we may not be able to settle this, ever. The word may really be vague, so that any attempt to pin down its literal meaning any more precisely is bound to fail. Further, even if all antiques are valuable, it could be that they are valuable because they are antiques, being antiques only because of their age. And if they are valuable because they are antiques they can hardly be antiques because they are valuable, can they?

Exercise 717

Reason: Poor Mary had a stroke.
Conclusion: Something went wrong with the blood supply to her brain.

Note that this is only one sense of this ambiguous word. In other senses it would mean that she swung a golf club or an oar. Back to the medical sense: It does not follow that there is anything wrong with her now. This may be so, and may be an inevitable consequence of what went wrong with her brain, but if it is a consequence at all it is a medical consequence not a logical one.

Exercise 718

Reason: Hamish plays the bagpipes.
Conclusion: He plays a musical instrument.

One thing that does not follow is that he is a Scot, despite the name. The pipes he plays may be from some other place, in fact, and as far as the meaning of the term is concerned could be from anywhere. Furthermore, even if the pipes were always Scottish and only played by Scots, they would not suddenly cease to be bagpipes if a Sassenach was to play them.

Exercise 719

Reason: Eric drives a pre-1930 car.
Conclusion: He drives an old car.

It does not follow that he does not drive a new car. He may drive more than one. Not at once probably, but here "drive" is used dispositionally.

Exercise 720

> Reason: Mr Martin is a prudent fellow.
> Conclusion: He is unlikely to act without weighing up the
> consequences.

Although the picture comes to mind of a cautious person, this does not follow. The prudent Mr Martin may decide that the probable consequences require that he act boldly.

Exercise 721

> Reason: Janice promised to give it back.
> Conclusion: She gave her word.

You think I am being cautious? You think that it follows that she ought to give it back? But just suppose that in the intervening period she has died? In that case she cannot give it back, and so how can it be the case that she ought to?

Exercise 722

> Reason: The forecast is for fine weather.
> Conclusion: The meteorologists say that it will be fine.

You think that I am being too cautious again? Well this time I believe I am rather incautious - the forecast might be issued by the tea-lady or the boot-boy. And as to the inference that it will indeed be fine, that is certainly not a logical consequence of the reason given.

Exercise 723

> Reason: Louis is saving up for a Stradavarius.
> Conclusion: He is saving up for a musical instrument.

We could be much more precise, but it does not follow that he is saving up for a violin, in the modern sense of that word. Stradavari also made violas and cellos, and the term applies to any instrument he made.

Exercise 724

> The Volga river flows through Auckland and on through Mexico City
> to the sea. So Auckland must be higher than Mexico City.

Do not expect to find something "deep" in each of these exercises. Just look for what is there, and comment accordingly.

Here the relation in question, if there is any meaning-relation behind the inference, is between "flows" and "higher". The trouble is that we can all imagine cases where water proceeds uphill, and if we watch firemen at work we do not even have to imagine it. There is no reason at all why we should not call this "flowing". So, although it may have appeared that the inference does depend for its validity upon the relation between the meanings of "flow" and "higher", it cannot be as simple as that. If there is a relation between "flow" and "higher" it is not - dare I say this? - a watertight one. To say it is flowing perhaps gives support to the statement that it is moving downhill, but this does not necessarily follow.

Notice though that this is about rivers, and perhaps they are necessarily open, unlike pipes and hoses. But that does not suffice to establish a strong semantic connection, even between flowing-in-rivers and going downhill. Near where I live there is a river which discharges into the sea, and twice a day the water flows uphill in this river as the tide rises.

Exercise 725

> Plato maintained that knowledge of the everyday mundane world is not true knowledge, as this world is a mere shadow or reflection of the true world, the World of Forms.

Danger, Philosophers at Work! (Some would say, at play.)

A serious warning. Philosophers are specially apt to draw inferences which depend for what validity they have upon the meanings of the words they use. (Indeed, one wonders how else they could ply their trade.)

For outsiders (at least) one difficulty is that this is likely to be done in idiosyncratic ways (that is, key words get used in special senses which are unfamiliar and change from philosopher to philosopher). It is also likely to be systematic, so that when you are on page 749 you have to remember the precise details of the way "mundane" was last used - page seventeen if only you can find it!

Still, you may try a bold approach and maintain that you do not have the faintest idea what is being claimed. And back up this (safe) contention by saying that you do not know what it is to distinguish between one world and another. As far as you are aware there is only one world, the world, and until Plato gives you some compelling reason for abandoning this reasonable position you will not feel obliged to attach any sense to his remarks.

Notice how, by attending to what looks like a departure from the common sense of a word we have called the whole project into question. If you feel more at home amongst sceptical philosophers than amongst speculative ones, this is a device you will often be tempted to employ, against the speculators.

Exercise 726

> You cannot have that. It is mine.

If you want to exploit the full range of meanings here, at one extreme you can construe it so that it looks like a fully valid argument. This is when "You cannot have that" is taken to mean "It cannot be the case that you own that."

But wait: even here the conclusion does not follow. "It is mine" does not entail that it is not also yours. Joint ownership is not logically impossible. So even on this extreme interpretation, the inference is by no means fully supported by the meanings of the words used.

And anyway it is unlikely that this would be the intended sense of "You cannot have that". A pedant would insist that the conclusion be expressed "You may not have that", meaning "You should not take that". Here there is some support from the meanings of the words. In calling this thing mine I do thereby come close to saying that you ought not take it from me.

I am not pretending to provide a philosophical analysis of these concepts, but I hope these exercises are helping to show how important it is to be sensitive to meanings.

Exercise 727

> Being unable to see, bats have to use a form of radar to avoid obstacles when flying.

I have already mentioned the point that it is sonar, not radar, as bats use sound waves rather than radio waves.

We must grant that there is a point here. But it is a fine point. There is no reason why we should restrict our use of the word "radar" to devices that use electromagnetic waves, even if the experts do this. The word is no longer a purely technical term, and if we want to use it as a generic term for anything which operates on certain geometrical principles, we may. That way we can regard sonar as a form of radar.

My reference to geometrical principles is deliberate. Modern conceptions of vision (unlike some older ones) regard it as a matter of reception of light which has reflected off the object seen but whose source typically is independent of the seer. Radar and sonar involve sending out waves as well as receiving them. Thus they work on geometric principles quite different from those involved in seeing.

But this is not to say that the inference is supported by relations between meanings. To see does not mean to operate that way, geometrically.

Exercise 728

It must have been John who ate that last piece of cake - he cannot resist it.

There is a connection in the meanings here, and that is what makes us want to say that this is a good inference. Which it most certainly is not: perhaps Trev cannot resist it either, or Eric, or Mary, or Roy, but it does not follow that all of them ate it, or indeed that any of them ate it. We need to know not only that John cannot resist it but also that he and it were suitably placed in time and space for this inability to manifest itself.

The connection in meanings is that a person who cannot resist cake typically eats it when it is available. The argument is not a good one, simply because it does not say or show that it was available, available to John and not available to anyone else with this same weakness for cake.

Exercise 729

We give you the best deal in town because we guarantee to match any firm's regular price on any of our lines.

If "best" means as good as anyone else then this may be a fair inference - provided the restriction to "our" lines is not too restrictive. But it is no better than a fair inference, because all it ensures (more or less) is best equal position, and that is hardly the best. If we take "best" strictly, as better than anyone else, then the inference is a poor one. You have to do more than match a price to give a better deal.

Exercise 730

A private commercial college can offer courses for as little as $3500 per year and make a tidy profit. The real cost per course in the university system is three times this sum. The conclusion is obvious - our universities are inefficient and should be sold off into private owner-ship.

This trades on a use of "inefficient" which is so far from what the word normally means that it must rank as a misuse - a confusion of cheapness for inefficiency. The reasons establish (if true) that commercial colleges do what they do more cheaply than universities do what they in turn do. For anything interesting to follow we should also be told that they both do the same job. This may be true, but it has to be stated.

Exercise 731

> The occasional setback is good for us, because it reminds us that anything worth having is worth fighting for, and helps us to set clear goals.

This sort of argument appears daily in the newspaper letters, in official speeches. It seems that this is a special form of talking that people learn so that they will not have to think?

How do meanings come in? Well the trouble really is that they don't. The language is extremely vague, and so when we try to do our usual appraisal we do not know what it is that we are appraising.

The thing to do at that stage is stop. If a passage is too vague to appraise it is too vague to appraise.

Exercise 732

> Too much aspirin is bad for your digestion. When you have a headache you should take something else.

One sad thing about examples like this is that you do not have to make them up - keep your ears open and you will hear them every day.

I trust you know how to handle the "too much" move? The amount you need to fix the headache may not be too much, may have no effect upon your digestion at all, but unless it does have this effect the argument is no good at all.

Often though when words like "too much" are used, they are not used to mean "too much", simply. The are used in a context, a context in which (say) somebody is taking aspirin and is taking what in the opinion of someone else is too much. And in these circumstances, the argument may be fine.

So the passage used in this exercise may have been used to express this:

You have been taking over twelve aspirin a day for your headaches, and that number will damage you kidneys, so you should find some other way of relieving the headaches.

That is a much better argument.

Exercise 733

As all energy changes are at least to some extent irreversible, it follows that the entropy of the universe must be continuously increasing. Eventually it will attain its maximum, and then the universe will reach its heat death - no more energy will be available to do work.

There are some subtle problems with meanings here. This is an attempt to state in more or less everyday English one of the fundamental laws of Physics. One problem is that terms which are rather imprecise in everyday language take on more precise and sometimes rather different meanings in science. "Heat", "energy", and "work" are the obvious ones here.

Then there are the fully technical terms - "entropy". Yes we can look them up in a dictionary, but unless we have studied a goodly chunk of the science concerned we are likely to have only a shadow of an idea of what they mean.

If you do know the physics you could go on and explain how the meanings of "entropy" and "energy" and "heat" and "work" are related. If you do not know the physics I think you would be wise to say so, and use that as an excuse for silence. It is a good enough excuse.

Exercise 734

This land was more or less empty when my ancestors arrived here. They took over only what they needed and developed it to serve those needs, clearing bush for their farms, building roads and bridges and towns and cities. It is ludicrous to suggest that it must all be returned to the previous inhabitants. It has become our property by virtue of the improvements made by generations of hard-working and God-fearing settlers.

One set of related meanings at work here is the idea of property and the idea of being entitled to possession. Undoubtedly the statement that this is John's property does entail, other things being equal, that he is entitled to it.

But the real work in the passage is done through the idea that one can acquire property in a certain way, by taking over something that is not obviously being used and improving it. And that is a moral theory. (I think it comes to us from John Locke.)

The question is - is this an acceptable moral theory or is it not? (Recall the Important New Technique in the Model Answers to Chapter 6 - no 613.) I do not think that it is, and for that reason I must reject the inference that assumes this theory.

Exercise 735

> It is a mistake to allow our schools to cater for what the pupils want. What matters is not what they want but what they need, and we adults must be the judges of that. More than ever, today's children need to master basic language and mathematical skills. The curriculum must concentrate upon these, however unpopular they may be.

Here we could get into a philosophical debate, about wants and needs. And that would be a good idea - it is exactly what we need to do, even if it is not what we want to do, if we are going to sort this one out. The argument hinges on this distinction, and if we are to evaluate the argument we should make sure that we understand the distinction.

Of course the argument hinges on other things too. We could grant the distinction but not the inference. But remember when you start tearing it to pieces, one of the reasons states that adults must be the judge of what children need. If you disagree with that you are disagreeing only with one of the reasons, not with any of the inferences. And as a logician your concern is first with the inferences, not the reasons.

Exercise 736

> If we are going to provide free education for the young we should also provide it for anyone else who wants it.

Although stated as a simple conditional this is easily construed as an argument, with the unstated reason that it would be wrong or ridiculous to provide free education for anyone who wants it and the unstated conclusion that it is wrong or ridiculous to provide free education for children.

That argument is formally valid. The mistake is in accepting the stated reason, in accepting that if we do the one then of necessity we will also have to do the other. For of course we do not. There is a host of ways we might defend the practice of providing free education for children but only for children.

This sort of argument is called a *slippery slope.* A slippery slope argument invites us to accept that if we assent to one statement we have to assent to another. The way to cope with a slippery slope is to dig your toes in. Unless a compelling, independent reason is given, it is always open to us to accept the first statement but refuse the second.

Exercise 737

> There never has been any direct and positive proof that electrons actually exist. What we are shown are always the so-called effects of electrons, never the electrons themselves. Clearly, they are purely figments of the physicist's underemployed imagination.

There is no proof that such-and-such is true, therefore it is false. That is so palpably invalid that it is difficult even to say just what is wrong with it. The conclusion simply does not follow. To use one of the traditional Latin phrases, this is a simple *non sequitur* ("it does not follow"). And to use the phrase which is specially reserved for this type of *non sequitur* - this is a case of *argumentum ad ignorantiam* ("argument appealing to ignorance").

(A note to anyone who thinks that the important thing is to learn these new technical terms - It isn't! The important thing is to use the techniques you already know to expose mistakes in reasoning. These fallacy-names are an optional extra. After all, there is no point in saying that an inference commits the fallacy of *argumentum ad ignorantiam* unless you can explain just what has gone wrong which entitles you to use the impressive phrase, and then, if you can indeed explain, you do not need the phrase.)

Exercise 738

> Fascism cannot be anything like as bad as it is made out to be. Look how many ordinary sensible Germans joined the Nazis, and were prepared even to die, fighting for a Fascist society.

Lots of people thought it was all right, so it must have been! The argument assumes that these people were not mistaken. Which could be wrong, so the argument is fallacious. Any number of people - even ordinary sensible Germans - can be deceived.

This is an example of *argumentum ad populum* - appealing to the opinions of the multitude. Of course we are wise to be guided by the opinions of large numbers of ordinary sensible people, but only when we have good reason to believe that they are not mistaken. The statement that lots of people believe something does not show that it is true, however many people are involved.

Exercise 739

> If you don't attend all of the classes and submit the essays on time you
> will fail. Anyone who is interested in the course will be prepared to do
> the work required, and if you aren't interested there is no way I can
> pass you.

Anyone interested will do the work (stated reason). If that is accepted, it follows
that anyone who does not do the work is not interested. And anyone not
interested will not pass (stated reason). Hence (presumably) they will fail. So
it follows that anyone who does not do the work will fail. Which is the stated
conclusion (first sentence). But wait. The reason mentions doing the work
required, while the conclusion mentions doing all of the work. If the arguer
thinks that these are the same, then the very *question* at issue is being *begged.*
The argument assumes the crucial part of what it sets out to establish - an
example of the fallacy of begging the question, or - in Latin - *petitio principii.*

If on the other hand the arguer does not simply assume that all of the work is
required, then a statement to this effect has to be added to the reasons, if the
conclusion is to follow. And such a statement, coming from an examiner, can
be seen as a threat. Arguments which try to force us to accept a conclusion
by threatening dire consequences if we don't are said to commit the fallacy of
argumentum ad baculum ("appealing to the cudgel"). Like *ad populum*, this is
one of the *fallacies of relevance*, where the truth of the reasons is not relevant
to that of the conclusion.

Note though that as is so often the case, this appraisal depends upon the
interpretation of the passage, in particular upon taking the first sentence as
the conclusion. Other interpretations are possible, and will call for different
appraisals.

Exercise 740

> There is nothing inherently wrong with warfare. Sure, it involves
> killing people, but when your life is threatened you are no longer
> required to respect the lives of others.

Another impressive Latin fallacy-title - *secundum quid.* Otherwise known as
the *converse fallacy of the accident.*

In more familiar terms, what is wrong with this argument is that it assumes
that warfare is always or inherently a matter of self defence. Would that it were
- then it would necessarily be rare. The converse fallacy of the accident is

defined as inferring an unqualified principle from a qualified one. Here the qualified principle is about self defence only, while the unqualified one is about all warfare, whether defensive or aggressive. Even if warfare-in-self-defence is all right, it does not follow that warfare-in-general is all right.

I think that this example clearly shows the superiority of our general method of appraising arguments. It is quite clear what this argument assumes. And it is quite clear that it will be false as often as it is true. No technicalities are needed here.

Exercise 741

Tom Smith is a real bad egg. All of the trouble-makers end up as union officials, and he has just been elected secretary of the Drivers' Union.

Compare these two argument forms:

All As are Bs; this is a B; so this is an A.
All As are Bs; this is an A; so this is a B.

The latter is clearly valid. But the argument about Tom Smith is an example of the first form, and that is clearly fallacious. It is known as the fallacy of the *undistributed middle*. "Distributed" is a technical term from traditional syllogistic logic (another technical term). I will not try to explain it here. Instead I will show that the form is fallacious by constructing another example of this same form and which has true reasons but a false conclusion:

All of the kings of England were male.
Atilla the Hun was male.
Therefore Atilla the Hun was a king of England.

The first reason is true, and so is the second one, but the conclusion is false. So "undistributed middle" is a fallacious argument form.

In practice, I do not think there is much point in remembering the phrase "undistributed middle". Whenever you come across an example you can easily show that it is fallacious by constructing a *counterargument*, as I have just done.

Exercise 742

No Western European nation could hope to mount a successful military attack on the USSR, so the Soviet Union has nothing serious to fear from Western Europe.

No Western nation on its own could mount a successful attack. That is all that the stated reason states. Accepting that, does it follow that Western Europe cannot mount one? No, of course it doesn't. Acting together, the nations of Western Europe might well achieve what no nation on its own could achieve. Often a whole class is capable of actions which are well beyond the powers of any individual member of the class.

This argument commits what is known as the *fallacy of composition* - arguing that what is true of the parts of some whole or class is thereby true of the whole or class itself. Of course it may be true of the whole, but not for that reason.

Exercise 743

> I wouldn't listen to what Harry says about repairing cars if I were you. Just look at his! It must be all of fifteen years old, and it's always giving him trouble. And everyone knows that he drinks far too much.

We can easily imagine a case where these reasons are true but the conclusion is false - where he is a heavy drinker and does have a troublesome old car but is nevertheless an expert at repairing cars. So the reasoning is fallacious. Indeed it is so bad that one hesitates to call it reasoning at all. Instead of giving us reasons for believing that the conclusion is true this passage mounts a personal attack, an irrelevant personal attack. It is an example of the fallacy of *argumentum ad hominem* (directed at the person), another fallacy of relevance.

Exercise 744

> If you chop that tree down there will be another drought this summer. Didn't they teach you at school that trees increase the rainfall?

We have met an example of the fallacy of composition. This is the opposite - the *fallacy of division* - where what is true of a whole class is said thereby to be true of individual members of the class. No individual tree can produce enough rainfall to prevent a drought - that requires lots of trees. While it may be true that each and every tree can and does have some effect upon precipitation, it is not thereby preventing a drought.

Of course this argument can quite easily be improved, the fallacy can be avoided. But as it stands it is a most unreliable inference.

Exercise 745

> There was none of this gang violence and rape when I was young and people still went to Church!

Post hoc ergo propter hoc - "after this therefore on account of this". The Latin fallacy-name is rather impressive, and the translation is informative - what else has to be said? In the vast majority of cases where A precedes B, A has nothing to do with causing B. To establish a causal connection we need to find out a lot more about A and B.

Exercise 746

> You must agree that my answers are the correct ones. After all I am the examiner, and if you answer incorrectly I will be forced to fail you.

Petitio principii - the question (whether your answers are the correct ones) is begged when in the reason it is implied that if my answer is not the one you want then mine is incorrect.

Equivocation - that is, using a word in one sense in the reasons but in another in the conclusion. Clearly this is an improper move in reasoning, a fallacy. In this case the equivocation is on "correct" - between what the examiner says is correct and what is correct. These may not be the same, but the argument uses the word "correct" so as to close off this possibility, incorrectly.

Argumentum ad baculum - a thinly veiled threat that if you don't answer the way I want you to there will be dire consequences. Of course the threat may be justified, even reasonable, but it is not a reason for accepting that my answers are correct.

Exercise 747

> All of the top managers in the company wear grey suits and white shirts and black shoes, so if you want to get to the top you had better follow their example.

They all dress that way right now, granted. But what about tomorrow? Are we given any reason for believing that they will be as dull tomorrow as they are today? No, there is nothing in the argument which gives any support at all to this proposition. (Of course there may be such reasons, but that is beside the point.) And that is exactly what we need to know if we are to infer the conclusion. In terms of unstated reasons, we need to add a statement to the effect that it will continue to be the case that the top managers all wear grey suits etc. If it does continue to be so, and you do not wear one, then certainly you will not be one of them.

That is one approach. Another is to point out that it has not been shown or even stated that dressing this way is a necessary condition of becoming a top manager. It may be accidental that they all dress that way - just as they may all happen to have birthdays in January. (Use that possibility to construct a counter-argument which is clearly invalid.) For this reason, this could be called an example of the *fallacy of false cause* - where some universal but possibly accidental feature is taken without sufficient reason to be part of a cause.

Exercise 748

> Freud's entire theory of human sexuality has been exposed as worth-
> less, as no more than the drug-induced fantasy of a cocaine addict.

This is a case of *argumentum ad hominem*, and a particularly invidious variety, where the origins of some idea are taken to be relevant to its truth. The reason in this passage may well be true, and so indeed may the conclusion, but the reason offers no support whatsoever for the conclusion. Of course we do well to treat with suspicion the drug-induced fantasies of cocaine addicts, when they lay claim to scientific respectability, but we are not entitled thereby to dismiss them as false or worthless.

Exercise 749

> I never had a single day sick in bed until I moved here to Auckland. It
> must be a really unhealthy place.

If it is a really unhealthy place we would expect to find a disproportionate number of sick people there. But we don't. So even if the reason is true, the conclusion isn't, and so the inference is fallacious.

This is called the fallacy of *hasty generalisation*, a name which scarcely needs explaining.

Exercise 750

> Surely there must be some truth in astrology! Countless wise people
> have believed in it over the centuries, and have been prepared to
> entrust the entire running of their lives to the influences of the
> heavenly bodies.

The use of the word "countless" makes this an example of *argumentum ad populum*.

The use of the word "influences" makes this an example of *petitio principii* - what is in question is precisely whether there are any such influences.

And the use of "wise" perhaps contributes to another fault - an illicit *appeal to authority*. Of course if they really were wise and if they knew that there are no such influences they would not have relied upon them. On the other hand if they really were wise and knew that there are such influences they would have relied upon them. (So the word "wise" too contributes to a *petitio principii*.) The point I want to make is that often an argument cites irrelevant qualifications, and that could be so here. For of course even a wise person might not know. An appeal to authority is fine if the authority appealed to is an authority in the right field. But that is not what is going on in this argument, I suspect.

Improving an Argument 8

So far we have concentrated upon the various ways that an argument can go wrong. But it is important to be able to produce a good argument too, not only to criticise a bad one. In this chapter, therefore, we will get in some practice at improving an argument.

Here are four useful "headings":

> *Clarity* - Is the argument expressed as clearly as possible? Can it be improved by rewriting?

> *Reliability* - Are the main inferences reliable? Can the argument be changed so as to improve their reliability and still support the main conclusions?

> *Plausibility* - Are the reasons and conclusions plausible? Can they be made more plausible?

> *Other reasons* - Does the argument mention all of the relevant reasons? Are there other lines of reasoning which should be added?

Clarity

By now you will realise that it is important to make sure that any vagueness and ambiguity is attended to. Feel free to rewrite a passage if it is unclear. After all, an argument is a series of statements, not sentences. If the actual sentences used to make an argument are not clear, then it is not clear exactly what is being argued. Until that is clear, there is little point in doing anything with the argument.

Apart from ambiguity and vagueness, there are other unclarities which can stand in the way of argument analysis and improvement. Poor construction of the passage, repetition, inclusion of irrelevant words and phrases, for example. Also exaggeration, and understatement. All of these should be attended to. This means again that it will often be necessary to rewrite the argument.

Reliability and Plausibility

A *sound* argument is one with *valid* inferences and *true* reasons. An argument which falls short of this ideal can be improved if its inferences can be made more reliable or if its reasons and conclusions can be made more plausible.

These two features are connected.

It is often possible to "beef up" the inferences - to turn a weak inference into a strong one, or a strong inference into a valid one. This as you have already seen can be done in a variety of ways - by adding extra reasons, by weakening conclusions.

For example, we have had a lot of practice with the "unstated reasons" method. Two rather different sorts of case emerge.

Sometimes the unstated reasons are not at all probable, even given the stated reasons. If this is the case, although the inference becomes more reliable if we add the unstated reasons, it would be silly to do this. We can make the inference stronger by adding the unstated reasons, but only at the expense of producing an argument which contains implausible reasons. There is nothing much we can do to improve this sort of argument.

The other sort of case is where the unstated reasons are quite probable. Here there is no objection to adding them to the argument. Indeed, we should add them. As before, the inference is strengthened, and this time the resulting argument does not contain any new implausibility.

In this sort of case we can often regard the unstated reasons as simple omissions from the stated argument, and by adding them we improve the argument. Indeed, this is what we have been doing all along. Strictly speaking, an argument which has some of its important reasons unstated cannot be highly reliable, even if the unstated reasons are true. Strictly, it is only the argument we get by stating those unstated reasons that is a highly reliable one. But often the unstated reasons are being taken for granted. They may be such common knowledge that they go without saying. If you think that this is what is going on, you should simply add these unstated reasons and assess the expanded argument. If something goes without saying it is petty to criticise anyone for not saying it.

An example:

> *Phenodon punctatus* is a reptile, so it is cold-blooded.

Even without knowing what sort of reptile *phenodon punctatus* happens to be, or even whether it is in fact a reptile at all, we know the unstated reason: All reptiles are cold-blooded. And this is true, so it does no harm to add it to the argument.

On the other hand, consider:

> *Phenodon punctatus* is a reptile, so it has four legs.

This assumes that all reptiles have four legs, which is wrong. Snakes have no legs at all (and turtles have flippers). So if we add this reason we do not thereby improve the argument. We start with an invalid argument with a true reason and a true conclusion, and end up with a valid argument with one false reason, one true reason and a true conclusion. Scarcely progress.

Another sort of case is where we can weaken a conclusion so as to make an inference more reliable. We have met cases like this:

> Poor Diana has the measles, so if you go near her you will catch it too.

The conclusion does not follow. All that does is that if you go near her you might catch it (ignoring other unstated reasons). But in many contexts that is all we would need to know. That is, the possibility of catching measles would be a good enough reason for staying away (and the unstated conclusion, here, is that you should keep away from her). Of course without a context we cannot be sure, but in some contexts at least it would be a distinct improvement to weaken the conclusion - "If you go near her you might catch it too" - producing a reliable argument whose conclusion says all we need to know.

Note that people do tend to overstate the conclusions of their arguments. Whenever you think that this has happened, it is a good idea to point this out and to weaken the conclusion accordingly.

A fourth case might now be occurring to you - where we strengthen an inference by strengthening the reasons. I do not mean the "unstated reasons" move, but the one analogous to weakening the conclusion. And indeed this move is sometimes open to us - where we are entitled to make stronger claims than are made by the stated reasons, thereby increasing the probability that the conclusion is true. Again, if you think that the reasons have been understated, it is a reasonable move to point this out and to strengthen them.

Other reasons

Does the argument mention all of the relevant reasons? Are there other lines of reasoning which should be added? Supplying other reasons for the conclusion is a powerful method of improving an argument when the argument is an explanation - when it is not a very good explanation, that is.

There are two rather different sorts of case. When the explanation is completely wrong, we need to replace the reasons. And when it is incomplete we need to add reasons until it is as complete as we can make it.

An example:

Diana's face is spotty because she has the measles.

If the stated reason is true, this is a fairly good explanation, which can be improved by adding the statement that people who have measles have spotty faces. We can make the explanation more complete by saying why that is so. On the other hand, if it is not universally true that people with the measles have spotty faces then we get a better explanation if we state precisely the conditions under which they do - and that these conditions apply in Diana's case.

If the stated reason is not true, though, we hardly improve the explanation by making additions like these. In this case we need to replace the reason with a statement of what is actually responsible for the spots - she has been playing with red paint, say.

Here is a diagram which represents some of the moves we might be able to make:

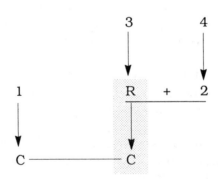

The original argument is from R to C: R for reason, C for conclusion.

The inference from 1 to C represents two possibilities:

(a)   Where 1 augments R.

If there are two independent lines of reasoning for a conclusion, and an argument states only one of them, it is an improvement if we add the other one.

(b)   Where 1 replaces R.

We decide that the stated reasons do not support the conclusion, but can think of other reasons which do support it. Of course this is an abandonment of the original argument rather than an improvement of it.

Adding statement 2.

This represents the standard "unstated reasons" case.

Adding reason 3.

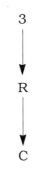

Particularly when we are dealing with an explanation, if we are able to push the reasoning back like this it is often an improvement.

Adding reason 4.

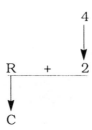

Again when the argument is an explanation, the unstated reasons are often general propositions, and if we can give some more basic reasons for accepting these then the argument is improved.

Returning to the example:

C/Diana's face is spotty/ <because> R/she has the measles/.

Statement 1 might be that she has been painting the ceiling red - and this may be either a supplement to R or an alternative. That is, she may have only paintspots on her face, in which case 1 replaces R, or she may have both paintspots and measles spots, in which case the argument should be depicted as convergent, with both 1 and R supporting C.

Statement 2 might be that measles makes your face spotty.

Statement 3 might be that she has been working next to Mary, who has the measles too (and statement 3a, linked in with 3, might be that measles is contagious).

Statement 4 might be some complex medical explanation of why measles gives you spots (and not, for example, stripes) on your face.

As you can see, the processes can be extended. Even with the additions, something important has been left out of the measles example. But I think there is enough detail to serve the purpose, which was to illustrate the main ways we can add reasons to an argument, thereby improving it.

EXERCISE EIGHT

Try to improve the arguments in these passages, using the methods mentioned in the chapter.

Explain your answers.

801 You shouldn't ever eat bananas - they are really bad for you. You see they contain a lot of calcium and that ruins your teeth. And remember they come from tropical countries where there are all sorts of exotic diseases.

802 Freud's entire theory of human sexuality has been exposed as worthless, as no more than the drug-induced fantasy of a cocaine addict.

803 We must stay a little longer. If we leave now we will offend your parents and we cannot afford to do that.

804 I have tossed this coin ten times and it came up "heads" only once, so it is almost certain to come up "heads" next time I toss it.

805 Do not lend your motorbike to Bill. Last time he rode one he crashed it, and anyway he's supposed to be mowing the lawns.

806 Even a very short vacation can be good for you, because it gives you a complete break from work. If you do not get away you end up a slave.

807 Too much aspirin is bad for your digestion. When you have a headache you should take something else.

808 We can't give the job to Fred. Don't you know he's an atheist? Every Sunday he goes off fishing - never to Church.

809 The kiwi cannot fly, having evolved in conditions where flying was not needed and where a heavy body was an advantage in digging deep for food. So over the years a series of heavier and heavier birds evolved with smaller and smaller wings, until the power of flight was lost completely.

810 If you drive with your foot resting lightly on the clutch pedal the clutch will wear out because the plates will be rubbing against each other.

811 I have been trying to fix the lawnmower all morning and now it is worse than it was when I started, so I might as well give up and use it as it is, if I can.

812 You have been driving with your foot resting against the clutch pedal and so the plates have been rubbing against each other. That is why the clutch is worn out.

813 Tomato plants should be tied onto stakes. It keeps the fruit off the ground.

814 It is a good idea to learn about other cultures. That way you come to realise how lucky you are.

815 Recent research strongly indicates that the fluorocarbons used as propellants in some aerosols destroy the ozone in the upper atmosphere. Since the ozone layer protects the Earth from harmful radiation, urgent steps must be taken to ban the use of these propellants.

816 The university system is in chaos. Both the Government and the University authorities are more concerned with holding on to power than with providing a good education for our young people. And the academics are no better. The only solution is to let the students take over.

817 You may have heard about mulching the garden. This is good in the spring because the mulch helps keep the soil moist in the summertime, and at the same time it prevents most weeds from germinating.

818 You must keep off the ice, because someone broke through yesterday and so it is dangerously thin.

819 Policemen walk a lot. That is why they have such large feet.

820 The bulb must have burned out - when I turn on the switch the light doesn't come on.

821 The old-fashioned method of designing a boat by making a solid wooden half-model and shaving off tiny pieces until it looks just right will no longer produce competitive yachts. A professional designer can eliminate hundreds of major variations by computer analysis and tank testing, so he has a formidable advantage over the traditional designer-builder.

822 When you raise the centreboard you reduce the yacht's lateral resistance, and one of the major heeling forces is provided by lateral resistance, so the yacht is less likely to capsize if you raise the centreboard.

823 Our hospitals are so full of drink-drive accident cases that you have to wait months and months for a simple operation. That is not good enough - we must do something to reduce the number of drinking drivers. The blood alcohol limit will have to be reduced - to zero.

824 Your car is ready for the junk yard, Tom. You can see the rust from the other side of the carpark, and the engine sounds dreadful.

825 Bread baked from stone ground organic wholemeal flour is far better for you than white bread because it contains no harmful residues.

826 You should wait a while before buying yourself a computer - prices have been dropping steadily for three years now, so they are sure to be even cheaper by this time next year.

827 Plant your vegetables in straight rows running North-South. That way you can keep them weeded and the sun can get to all of the plants.

828 We must stay a little longer. If we leave now we will offend your parents, and anyway the supper will be served soon and I am starving.

829 Medical care is, paradoxically, one of the major threats to the human species. Now that the major contagious diseases have been conquered, medical science will soon find effective cures for the degenerative diseases. When this happens, life expectancy will increase dramatically, food and housing resources will consequently become so inadequate that a major social breakdown will be inevitable.

830 Anna must have a very strong reason for throwing in her job. At her age you do not give up a good career in head office and vanish to some tiny country town. And nothing we can say will persuade her to come back, which suggests that somebody or something at head office was making her life intolerable.

EXERCISE EIGHT - MODEL ANSWERS

These model answers do not attend to all of the ways in which the argument concerned might be improved. You have probably been more systematic than I have, and so will have rather more detailed answers. Remember, though, that if an improvement is not a real improvement it is hardly worth mentioning.

Exercise 801

You shouldn't ever eat bananas - they are really bad for you. You see they contain a lot of calcium and that ruins your teeth. And remember they come from tropical countries where there are all sorts of exotic diseases.

Alternative reason - They make you fat. But adding this, on its own, is not an improvement unless we are prepared to accept that we should never eat anything that makes us fat. Here, I would weaken the conclusion - You shouldn't eat a lot of bananas.

The first stated reason is so obviously false that any form of renovation would be misguided.

The second argument, about disease, might be worth strengthening, again by weakening the conclusion so that all that is claimed is that it could be risky to eat bananas, and by adding the unstated reason which links the presence of exotic diseases with some risk to the consumer of bananas. Take care though that what you add is probable, or you have done little service to the argument.

Note that the conclusion has been weakened in two different ways. What conclusion could we accept if we now link the two acceptable lines of reasoning, rather than regard them as convergent?

(You will notice that I have not drawn a diagram. In simple cases like this it is scarcely worth while.)

Exercise 802

Freud's entire theory of human sexuality has been exposed as worthless, as no more than the drug-induced fantasy of a cocaine addict.

Alternative reason - It is based on unreliable data? But when an argument is as bad as this one I doubt whether any attempt at improving it is wise. Of course we may want to investigate both of the claims made - that Freud was an addict, and that his theory of sexuality is no good - but any attempt to forge a link between them would be a waste of time. Granted, there may be some general truths to learn about the opinions of addicts, but we already know how to assess a theory, and would be wise to apply the usual tests to Freud's, and these have nothing to do with whether he was an addict.

Exercise 803

> We must stay a little longer. If we leave now we will offend your parents
> and we cannot afford to do that.

This argument is so close to being valid that it leaves little room for improvement. It follows from the two stated reasons that we cannot afford to leave now, and the step from that to the stated conclusion is not a great one. The only way to avoid the conclusion is to deny that we must do something we cannot afford not to do. Not a great deal of room to move there.

The argument though can be strengthened by weakening the conclusion: change from saying that we must stay to saying only that it would be a pity or a mistake not to.

Exercise 804

> 1/I have tossed this coin ten times/ and 2/it came up "heads" only
> once/, <so> 3/it is almost certain to come up "heads" next time I toss
> it/.

A hard one to start with - this is so bad it is difficult to think of any worthwhile changes. (On the other hand, with a really bad argument almost any change will be worthwhile!) If there is anything that is supported by the reasons it would be this: that the coin is lopsided, out of balance, favouring the "tails" side. But that counts against the stated conclusion.

So, my response is that this is beyond help.

Exercise 805

> Do not lend your motorbike to Bill. Last time he rode one he crashed
> it, and anyway he's supposed to be mowing the lawns.

When you are dealing with a convergent argument you can treat the branches separately. And you need only bother with one of them, if you are lucky. That is, if one of the reasons offers strong enough support for the conclusion, you can do without the other line of argument.

Here, I am inclined to abandon the "right-hand" branch entirely - the one about mowing the lawns, which would be on the right-hand side of the diagram if we had one. I see no general connection between being supposed to mow lawns and borrowing a motorbike - indeed if the lawns are a long way away, the loan of a motorbike might help.

The other branch, though, is worth improving. One way of making it into a stronger inference is to weaken the conclusion. Instead of the unconditional: "Do not lend it to him", why not settle for the conditional "If you lend it to him he is likely to crash it"? The inference is still not valid but it is much better than it was.

To make it into a valid inference you would need another reason, such as "People who crash a motorbike once are likely to do so again". If that is true then it can be added.

Exercise 806

> 1/Even a very short vacation can be good for you/, <because> 2/it gives you a complete break from work/. 3/If you do not get away you end up a slave/.

This argument relies upon the true unstated reason that being a slave is not good for you. Add that and you have a very strong inference, if not a perfectly valid one.

Exercise 807

> Too much aspirin is bad for your digestion. When you have a headache you should take something else.

First we should remove the circularity from the stated reason. How many are bad for your digestion? More than twenty a day? Write that in instead - not that "too many" are bad for you but that more than twenty a day are.

Still it is not a good argument. If you have only occasional headaches, and one or two aspirins will fix them, then the fact that twenty a day is bad for the digestion is the least of your worries.

Exercise 808

> We can't give the job to Fred. Don't you know he's an atheist? Every Sunday he goes off fishing - never to Church.

Alternative reason (for the final conclusion) - He isn't qualified for the job. But we have such a bad argument here that it is scarcely worth bothering with it. Why seek alternative reasons for this conclusion, when we have been given no reason at all for accepting it? Indeed, the argument is so bad that the temptation is to look for reasons against the conclusion rather than for it.

Exercise 809

> 1/The kiwi cannot fly/, having 2/evolved in conditions where flying was not needed and where a heavy body was an advantage in digging deep for food/. <So> 3/over the years a series of heavier and heavier birds evolved with smaller and smaller wings, until the power of flight was lost completely/.

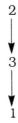

The inference from 3 to 1 is valid already.

The other one, from 2 to 3, assumes some form of evolutionary theory:

2a. An unused ability is likely to be lost.

The best thing to do is add this to the argument:

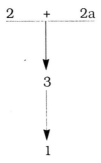

Now it is clear what general principle is being invoked, and as it is a well supported principle, the argument is improved when we add it.

Some people like to divide up a reason like 2. If you think that the argument can be improved by doing this, then do it.

Also - Look for alternative reasons. Maybe the kiwi never was able to fly. This is a possibility. Of course I don't believe that it is true, and so I wouldn't actually add it to the argument, but it is important to look for alternatives, even when the reasons you have seem quite good ones. This is how new explanations are discovered, or invented. A wasteful process, to be sure - very few new ideas turn out to be at all plausible in the long run - but this is an important way of helping to improve your powers of logical imagination.

And remember that it can be a mistake to reject a statement simply because you do not believe it to be true. For example, do you believe that the ancestors of dolphins were terrestial? I didn't when I was told this, but I was told by a biologist, and you would expect her to know more about this sort of thing than I do. So, even though I don't actually believe this, I would be foolish to reject it.

Exercise 810

> 1/If you drive with your foot resting lightly on the clutch pedal the clutch will wear out/ <because> 2/the plates will be rubbing against each other/.

This can be made into a valid inference by adding the statement that if the clutch plates rub against each other the clutch will wear out.

So - Should we add it? That depends upon whether it is probable. If it isn't, it hardly improves the argument. And that is as far as I can go, as I have no idea at all whether this is true or false. Sure, I have been told that it is so, but then again I have been told all sorts of amazing things, particularly about machines.

So my "answer" is this: Add that as an extra reason - if it is probable.

Also - Weaken the conclusion?

Exercise 811

> I have been trying to fix the lawnmower all morning and now it is worse than it was when I started, so I might as well give up and use it as it is, if I can.

There is an intermediate conclusion here, and it helps if it is stated explicitly:

The lawnmower is unlikely to get any better if I carry on trying to fix it.

This of course does not follow from the stated reason, without the help of other reasons. After all I might be one of those people who take a whole morning getting into a big mess and then suddenly it all comes right. But adding this intermediate conclusion does improve the clarity of the argument.

The second inference - from the unstated intermediate conclusion to the stated final conclusion - is a very poor one. After all, I might have a friendly neighbour who is an expert at fixing lawnmowers, in which case it would be dumb just to use it as it is. So here I am inclined to add the statement that there is no other way of getting the mower fixed. And of course the statement that I have to get the lawns done today, otherwise the sensible thing to do would be to forget both the lawns and the mower.

Exercise 812

1/You have been driving with your foot resting against the clutch pedal/ <and so> 2/the plates have been rubbing against each other/ <That is why> 3/the clutch is worn out/.

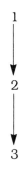

1

2

3

The inference from 1 to 2 relies on the statement that if you do drive this way the plates rub.

And the inference from 2 to 3 relies on the statement that if the plates rub the clutch is worn out.

You could then add both of these, if they are probable, and that would improve the argument.

On the other hand you could weaken both conclusions: first that the plates have probably been rubbing and second that the clutch is likely to be worn, or badly worn, or something like that.

Exercise 813

> Tomato plants should be tied onto stakes. It keeps the fruit off the ground.

Another reason - It eliminates places where slugs can hide. And perhaps this - Uncle James is a traditionalist and would be greatly upset if they were not tied up! But we cannot be expected to anticipate all circumstances. That is, we can only be expected to supply general reasons. And here, if we do see fit to add the reason about slugs, we must be careful not to use it instead of the stated reason.

Another way to improve this argument is to weaken the conclusion - say only that tomato plants should be provided with some form of support. This blocks off the obvious counterexamples, without requiring us to add a reason which is nowhere near true - say that the only way to keep them of the ground is to tie them onto stakes. We might have blocked the counterexamples that way, but unless there is good reason to believe that the stated argument is definitely about stakes - as opposed to other forms of support - it is better to weaken the conclusion than to add a dubious reason.

Exercise 814

> It is a good idea to learn about other cultures. That way you come to realise how lucky you are.

Remember what we found to be wrong with this argument before. If it is obvious that "you" do come from a privileged culture, then this statement can be added and the argument improved thereby, but don't forget that if this is not so, the realisation would likely be how unlucky you are.

Alternative reason - They are interesting, and more importantly, learning about them may make the lucky ones more sympathetic etc.

Exercise 815

> Recent research strongly indicates that the fluorocarbons used as propellants in some aerosols destroy the ozone in the upper atmosphere. Since the ozone layer protects the Earth from harmful radiation, urgent steps must be taken to ban the use of these propellants.

This is so close to being valid as it stands that you may have been tempted to leave well alone. There is room for improvement, though. First, it is not stated that the effects of the fluorocarbons are irreversible. If they are not, then no doubt we could try to reverse these effects rather than try to prevent them in the first place. So if it is indeed true that the effects are irreversible, it would improve the argument to add this statement.

Second, it does not follow from what is stated that this is an urgent matter. The ozone layer may be being destroyed at such a slow rate that we can afford to relax for a few million years. So again, if it is an urgent matter, this should be added as a reason. And if it is not, the conclusion should be weakened accordingly.

Exercise 816

> 1/The university system is in chaos/. 2/Both the Government and the University authorities are more concerned with holding on to power than with providing a good education for our young people. And the academics are no better/. The only solution is to 3/let the students take over/.

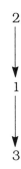

2

1

3

In Exercise 319 I included the whole of the final sentence in statement 3. And that is a reasonable reading. Here I have made a slight improvement by regarding the words "the only solution is to ..." as a rhetorical flourish rather than an integral part of the statement, and so even if there are other "solutions" we can still take the conclusion seriously. That is, by choosing the weaker version of the conclusion I have already made the argument as close to valid as I can, without real meddling.

Beyond this I am unsure what to do. The inference from 2 to 1 is very bad, and it is hard to think of any reasonable statement that could be added which would improve it. I mean, the inference depends upon a statement like "self interest always produces chaos", and I see no reason for accepting that.

The second inference depends upon the assertion that the students have an interest in running the university properly, and will be able to do this. I think that this should be added. Is is clearly what would be intended in any imaginable context in which the argument would be seriously employed, and it is not ridiculous.

Exercise 817

You may have heard about mulching the garden. 1/This is good in the spring/ <because> 2/the mulch helps keep the soil moist in the summertime/, and at the same time 3/it prevents most weeds from germinating/.

The inference from 2 to 1 depends upon the unremarkable proposition that it is good to keep the garden moist in the summertime. Except for those who carefully cultivate dustbowls this is likely to be true and so we can happily add it. We might also add that the garden needs keeping moist in the summer, so as to make it clear that the argument is not meant to refer to places with wet summers rather than dry ones.

The inference from 3 to 1 also depends upon an innocent sounding proposition - that it is a good thing not to have weeds germinating in your garden. This is very close to being true by definition - a weed being defined as anything that shouldn't be there. So except for energetic and diligent souls who feel they have not done their garden justice unless they have hoed out a few weeds each day - these ones of course need to have some weeds germinating so that they can hoe them - we can happily add this statement too.

And there could well be other reasons involving soil structure, micro-organisms, etc.

Exercise 818

1/You must keep off the ice/, <because> 2/someone broke through yesterday/ <and so> 3/it is dangerously thin/.

The person who broke through might have jumped from a great height to do so, the ice might now be much thicker than it was yesterday, and so on. The first inference is a bad one, and unless we are confident that none of these conditions obtain, there is little that can be done to improve it.

The second is better. Add the statement that you do not want to break through, and it is quite a good inference.

Exercise 819

Policemen walk a lot. That is why they have such large feet.

Alternative reason - You have to be tall to be accepted as a policeman, and tall people tend to have large feet anyway.

But is it worthwhile adding this? The result would be an argument where one reason contradicts the other. If on the other hand we replace the original reason with the new one, we have abandoned the original argument, not improved it. In my opinion the original argument is so wrong-headed that it is rather pointless to try to fix it up at all.

Exercise 820

The bulb must have burned out - when I turn on the switch the light doesn't come on.

Alternative reason - The power has been turned off at the mains. If this is clearly not so - say the heater is still going - then it improves the argument to add it. But there are other alternative reasons which cannot easily be checked.

Exercise 821

The old-fashioned method of designing a boat by making a solid wooden half-model and shaving off tiny pieces until it looks just right will no longer produce competitive yachts. A professional designer can eliminate hundreds of major variations by computer analysis and tank testing, so he has a formidable advantage over the traditional designer-builder.

I am told by people who know nothing about boat design that this argument seems to be a convincing one. Good - it was meant to seem that way. But I assure you it is not a good one at all. It depends upon the assumption that the aim is to produce a fast yacht. Granted, the new methods are what you need for this, but if you want to produce a good looking one then there is nothing wrong with the old way. And although "competitive" may seem to suggest "fast", amongst say yacht builders it could mean one that will outsell the opposition, and here the looks may be more important than the performance.

What I think we should do is make it explicit that this argument is about designing fast ones, by making the conclusion more explicit and also conditional: A professional designer has a formidable advantage over the traditional designer-builder in producing fast yachts.

Note that the argument does not show that the new methods always produce competitive yachts. That would be a much harder conclusion to establish, as it is false.

Exercise 822

> 1/When you raise the centreboard you reduce the yacht's lateral resistance/, and 2/one of the major heeling forces is provided by lateral resistance/, <so> 3/<u>the yacht is less likely to capsize if you raise the centreboard</u>/.

I hope that as you get in more and more practice with arguments from fields about which you are relatively ignorant you are becoming more and more confident of making a reasonable appraisal of the arguments. And of course as I said in Chapter Three about this very example, a moment with a dictionary will often help.

It follows from 1 and 2 that when you raise the centreboard you reduce one of the major heeling forces (no don't take my word for it - check that this does follow). Does it then follow that the yacht is less likely to capsize? Well, provided that the smaller the heeling forces the less likely it is to capsize, this does follow. So that is what we should add - namely that the smaller the heeling forces the less likely the yacht is to capsize. (Of course if we know something about the field we might be able to demonstrate this, not just state it.)

This turns the argument into a valid one. I think it is also a sound one, but this is a tricky field, in which even professionals have been disastrously wrong, so I'll leave it at that.

Exercise 823

> Our hospitals are so full of drink-drive accident cases that you have to wait months and months for a simple operation. That is not good enough - we must do something to reduce the number of drinking drivers. The blood alcohol limit will have to be reduced - to zero.

The first inference is fairly good. It depends upon the statement that the number of drink-drive accident cases is directly related to the number of drinking drivers. This seems to be a reasonable assumption to make, so I would add this statement as a reason just to make everything perfectly clear.

The second inference is not a good one, though. It has to be said that this is the only way of achieving the result. But that is quite possibly false. Several other measures might well reduce the number of drinking drivers. And while the blood alcohol limit will probably have to be reduced, it will not necessarily have to be reduced to zero.

Exercise 824

> 1/Your car is ready for the junk yard, Tom/. 2/You can see the rust from the other side of the carpark/, and 3/the engine sounds dreadful/.

First problem: is this linked or convergent? Well here our job is to improve the argument if we can, so our duty is clear - represent it as being linked rather than convergent, as that in itself will almost always produce a better argument (the exception being when one of the reasons does not support the conclusion in any way at all). Thus, to interpret the argument as charitably as possible we should choose the right-hand diagram as the structure.

Still, this is not a very impressive argument. Let us grant that rust and noisy engines are bad things in cars (add that as another reason), we still do not know whether Tom's car should be scrapped or fixed. So we have to say that it is beyond repair, if we want the conclusion to follow.

Does that follow from the reasons stated? I do not think so. It all depends, surely, upon the relative cost and/or ease of repairing a car versus replacing it. (Assuming that Tom wants a car. If he doesn't then the argument for fixing it is much weaker, but now he might as well abandon it as scrap it, perhaps.)

So, here I would add the statement that rust and noisy engines are bad, and I think that I would add the dubious statement that Tom's car is beyond repair.

Exercise 825

> Bread baked from stone ground organic wholemeal flour is far better for you than white bread because it contains no harmful residues.

Another reason - It contains substances which are good for you and are not present in white bread. This is true, and should be added, as a separate line of reasoning.

Another improvement to this argument is to weaken the conclusion. It certainly does not follow that the wholemeal bread is far better for you, even when the extra reason is added, so we should conclude only that it is better for you.

Exercise 826

> You should wait a while before buying yourself a computer - prices have been dropping steadily for three years now, so they are sure to be even cheaper by this time next year.

Alternative reason - Improved models will soon be available. And the inference depends upon the supposition that the fall in prices will continue. If this is an acceptable supposition, add it to the argument

Exercise 827

> Plant your vegetables in straight rows running North-South. That way you can keep them weeded and the sun can get to all of the plants.

Fair enough? Many people would say so, but now that we have learned to be very suspicious we should be able to think of cases where there are compelling reasons why North-South rows would be a bad idea. (Indeed by now it should be hard for us not to do this.) For example it might well be a bad idea to do,it on a North-South sloping hillside, where it would encourage erosion. This is one of those "other things being equal" arguments: The reasons stated support the statement that unless there are good reasons for doing something different, you should do this. And that is what I would do to improve the argument - add the words "other things being equal" to the conclusion. Then the erosion example is not a counterexample.

Exercise 828

> 1/We must stay a little longer/. 2/If we leave now we will offend your parents/, and anyway 3/the supper will be served soon/ and 4/I am starving/.

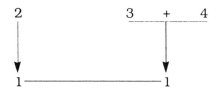

We know already how to improve the left-hand branch of this argument.

The right-hand branch depends upon the statement that starving is bad for me rather than good for me. If it is bad for me then perhaps we should restate 4 as "I need food urgently". That improves the inference. It does not make it valid of course - the food might all be poisoned.

Exercise 829

> 1/Medical care is, paradoxically, one of the major threats to the human species/. <Now that> 2/the major contagious diseases have been conquered/, 3/medical science will soon find effective cures for the degenerative diseases/. When this happens, 4/life expectancy will increase dramatically/, 5/food and housing resources will <consequently> become so inadequate/ that 6/a major social breakdown will be inevitable/.

(Excuse the non-standard diagram, but enough is enough.) Each inference can be dealt with separately. We might start by pointing out just how bad the inference from 2 to 3 is (although I am also tempted to regard all this as a single statement rather than an inference), and we might try to beef it up by adding some statement about how wonderfully successful Science is at solving new problems when it gets round to them (true or false?).

The next one, from 3 to 4, looks much better. Of course 4 does not follow logically - all sorts of new factors could counteract the effect (we might all take up mountaineering in the avalanche season, or suicide might become much more popular).

But all this is detail. To make much difference to this argument we have to work out what is the key move. Just how does the "paradox" get generated? Why blame medical science - rather than, say, fragile social institutions - for the predicted breakdown? Nothing in the argument says that medical science is to blame in any interesting sense of the word, even if it is a necessary condition.

So, if you want to strengthen the argument that medical science rather than say our social framework is a major threat you might also argue that there is nothing wrong with the social framework. That - if it could be done effectively - would be the sort of move that would make this argument much more compelling. (Is it worth the cost, though?)

Exercise 830

> 1/Anna must have a very strong reason for throwing in her job/. 2/ At her age you do not give up a good career in head office and vanish to some tiny country town/. And 3/nothing we can say will persuade her to come back/, <which suggests that> 4/somebody or something at head office was making her life intolerable/.

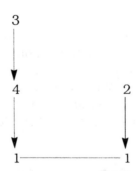

An easy one to end with - so easy that no doubt you have been looking for all sorts of subtle weaknesses in the argument. But here, apart from adding a rather obvious extra unstated reason I am inclined to leave this one alone. Why? Because it is already good enough, even with the convergent structure indicated.

What is the obvious unstated reason? Well I would add to 2 that she has done precisely this (and if you like point out that I am not taking the expression "no one" literally).

Pros and Cons   9

Most of the arguments we have met in this book have dealt with only one side of an issue - they have offered support for a particular conclusion but usually have given no idea of what reasons there may be against it.

But as you know, often we have to decide between competing reasons. There are reasons for believing a proposition and reasons against it - we have to sort out which are better, the pros or the cons.

Of course it is usually possible to treat them separately to start with, and it is often a good idea to do just this. That is, draw one diagram for the reasons in favour of the conclusion, and a separate diagram showing the reasons against. But sooner or later you have to ask which set of reasons is more persuasive, and for this you have to balance them against one another - you have to weigh up the pros against the cons. For this, it often helps if they are represented in a single diagram.

In this chapter we are going to develop techniques for doing just this, techniques for analysing reasons both for and against a conclusion - arguments which present both sides, arguments which rebut objections, and the like. The main technique is a simple one:

> When a reason is against a conclusion rather than in favour of it, draw a cross instead of an arrow head.

Here is a simple example:

> I know that Tom says we should go today, and he is the expert on fishing, but I say we have to wait until tomorrow, so that we can see Auntie Jane before she goes into hospital.

This presents reasons for and against a conclusion, and can be marked and diagrammed as follows:

> I know that 1/Tom says we should go today/, and 2/he is the expert on fishing/, but I say 3/we have to wait until tomorrow/, <so that> 4/ we can see Auntie Jane before she goes into hospital/.

Rewriting 4: We must see Auntie Jane before she goes into hospital.

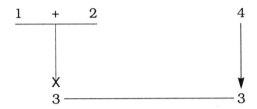

If you were to choose as conclusion the statement that we should go fishing today, then the pros here would become cons and the cons would become pros, but as the passage is written the conclusion being argued for is that we should wait until tomorrow.

You will realise that we do not have to use a single diagram. These two pictures tell the same story as the single one above:

Indeed, we can do without the cross-headed arrow. Let 5 be the statement that we should go fishing today, then the arguments run like this:

But in the following exercises, please construct a single diagram for each passage.

You will realise that there are no techniques here for working out whether the arguments in favour are better than the arguments against. All we have is a method of representing them on a single diagram. We still have to decide whether the pros outweigh the cons.

EXERCISE NINE

Numbers 901 to 905: Without disputing or denying the reasons stated, construct a good argument against the conclusion.

901 There is no need for anyone to learn mathematics any more. All that can be done on computers, now.

902 It is high time you got yourself a steady job, Tony. You will end up with no real skills if you carry on like this, and then when you want to settle down nobody will be willing to employ you.

903 No wonder we never get a good government. The trouble is we have elections far too often. The moment a party gets into office they have to worry about how we are going to vote next time.

904 If you really have to go hunting, make sure you wear brightly coloured clothes and make plenty of noise all the time. That way the other hunters should know where you are and what you are, so they are less likely to mistake you for a deer and shoot at you.

905 These aphids will ruin the tomatoes. They carry a virus disease which prevents the fruit from setting. So you will have to spray them straight away.

The passages below contain reasons against a conclusion as well as reasons for it. Construct a single diagram for each passage, using the cross-headed arrow for reasons against. Then assess the inferences.

906 You should take a coat, Jean. It is going to rain. See those dark clouds forming over the hills! That's a sure sign of rain - unless the wind swings to the south and clears them away, and they did say on the forecast there could be a Southerly change.

907 I wouldn't buy a car from that yard if I were you. They are an unscrupulous lot - even worse than the other dealers. Then again, they are by far the cheapest in town, so if that's what you want ....

---

908 Mary doesn't drink any more - not even beer. She joined the Baptists and they make you sign the pledge. Though from the look of her nose I wouldn't mind betting she still has the odd quiet one on the side.

909 I know that you are working very hard at your logic, Tony, but you really do not have a chance of getting to the top. All of the great logicians have been women.

910 I know that May is a bad time to go up North for a holiday, what with the storms and most of the hotels being closed, but if you don't get away now you'll have a breakdown. So off you go!

911 Unless there is a major breakthrough in computer technology - and I must say that on past performance the next one is already overdue - you should stick with your old machine for a few years. The newer models don't have any important advantages over it.

912 When you are writing your essay remember that the people who mark it are ordinary human beings like you and me. If you are lucky you will get credit for what you have done, whether the marker agrees or not, but all too often they just look to see whether you are saying what they want you to say.

913 It is a good idea to leave the catcher off the lawnmower. That way the clippings get left behind and they gradually break down and fertilise the lawn. Granted, they look untidy, and anyone walking inside will mess up the floors, but you will never have to put any of those chemicals on the lawn.

914 By far the best time to fish from the rocks is when the tide is rising. That's when the big ones come close inshore to feed. Of course you're far more likely to be swept away by a wave than you would be on a falling tide, but at least if you survive you should catch plenty.

915 All the experts say you should hold the bat straight when you are batting, but that way you can't get a good swing at the ball. No, unless you only want to survive for hours without scoring I reckon you should just hold the bat naturally, keep your eye on the ball, and swing across the line as much as you like.

916 Nobody is going to take you seriously as an artist unless you do "proper" paintings - big oils on stretched canvas. I realise that your best work is in the Japanese style - simple brushwork with black ink on paper - but when people round here pay for a painting they want it to look expensive.

Sorry Edith, but you have to cater for the market.

917 The trouble with a daisy-wheel printer is that it cannot do italics or expanded type or graphics. And it is terribly slow - you even have to feed in sheets of paper one at a time! But it produces much clearer copy than a dot-matrix printer, especially when you use carbon film ribbon, and that's important when you are trying to sell your work to a publisher.

918 I think you should tell them what you think about it Sue. Maybe they will treat you as a troublemaker. Maybe they will even turn nasty and fire you. But you have your self-respect to think of.

919 By using artificial fertilisers the farmers here have managed to boost production by up to eighty percent in the last ten years. Without that, many of them would be out of business. But the runoff is killing the fish in the streams and lakes, and now there is so much weed growing in the nitrogen-rich waters that the whole drainage system is endangered. Despite the benefits for production, this use of artificial fertiliser will have to stop - immediately.

920 Of course it is hard to let them have their way when you think they are being short-sighted, and of course you will blame yourself for the rest of your days if it ends in disaster, as you are predicting. But you have to let them make their own decisions. They are not children any more, and if you try to force them they will probably move out of town.

EXERCISE NINE - MODEL ANSWERS

Exercise 901

> There is no need for anyone to learn mathematics any more. All that can be done on computers, now.

Remember that we are not allowed to disagree with the reason stated. A good way of avoiding this is to think of a completely independent reason against the conclusion. One that comes to my mind is the claim that learning mathematics develops certain powers of the mind, which are useful elsewhere and perhaps even good in themselves. I am not sure how good an argument this is, but here goes:

> All of us need to learn some mathematics, not so that we can spend our time performing mathematical calculations - that can indeed be done by computers - but because learning mathematics develops our

powers of abstract thought, which is useful in many non-mathematical contexts and is perhaps even good in itself.

You see that I have followed orders and resisted the temptation to dispute the reason stated in the passage. Indeed, in my counter-argument I have even endorsed it, although in fact I might well want to take issue with it.

Exercise 902

It is high time you got yourself a steady job, Tony. You will end up with no real skills if you carry on like this, and then when you want to settle down nobody will be willing to employ you.

What sort of argument will count as a good argument here rather depends upon what sort of person Tony is, but we are told next to nothing about him and so are free to imagine him to be, say, so rich that he does not need to work, or so lucky .... So, for example:

You don't have to worry about getting a steady job, Tony. With all that money your uncle left you do not really have to work at all.

Exercise 903

No wonder we never get a good government. The trouble is we have elections far too often. The moment a party gets into office they have to worry about how we are going to vote next time.

The conclusion is that we never get a good government, so we are not allowed to dispute the statement that we have elections far too often, however strongly we disagree with it. What we have to do is think of reasons against the statement that we never get a good government which do not touch upon the frequency of elections. Which is not too hard a project, so long as we do not take too seriously the other requirement, that we produce a good argument.

Occasionally we do get a good government. Of course the electoral system makes this unlikely, but from time to time the nation becomes so united in its aims that almost anyone would be able to govern well. Particularly when there is some great national emergency, everyone knows what has to be done, and if the government does this they can be sure of getting re-elected.

Exercise 904

If you really have to go hunting, make sure you wear brightly coloured clothes and make plenty of noise all the time. That way the other hunters should know where you are and what you are, so they are less likely to mistake you for a deer and shoot at you.

I do believe that this really is one of those "no-win" situations! The argument to the contrary is obvious, and equally compelling:

When you go hunting you must wear very inconspicuous clothes and keep as quiet as possible if not quieter, or the game will know you are near and keep well away from you.

Exercise 905

These aphids will ruin the tomatoes. They carry a virus disease which prevents the fruit from setting. So you will have to spray them straight away.

This is such a bad argument that an argument against the conclusion is easy to find. For example:

Granted, the aphids will ruin the tomatoes, but that does not mean you have to fill the air with poisons. Instead, you could simply do without tomatoes.

Exercise 906

1/You should take a coat, Jean/. 2/It is going to rain/. 3/See those dark clouds forming over the hills/! 4/That's a sure sign of rain/ - 5/ unless the wind swings to the south and clears them away/, and 6/ they did say on the forecast there could be a Southerly change/.

Rewriting: 3. There are dark clouds forming over the hills.
            5. If the clouds are blown away by a southerly it will not rain.

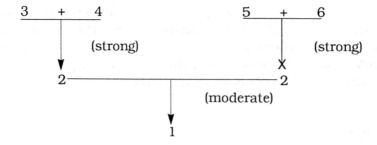

Note that the reasons against are directed against 2, not 1. Your diagram should show this clearly.

How good are the inferences? Well the inference from 2 to 1 is not very good. She may love getting wet. The others though are quite good. Of course the reasons cannot all be true. In particular, if the clouds are a sure sign of rain, not even a Southerly is going to prevent it. And conversely, if 5 as restated is true then clouds are not a sure sign of rain.

This is quite a common scene: We have good inferences both ways, and (therefore?) not all of the reasons can be true.

Exercise 907

1/I wouldn't buy a car from that yard if I were you/. 2/They are an unscrupulous lot/ - 3/even worse than the other dealers/. Then again, 4/they are by far the cheapest in town/, <so> 5/if that's what you want .../.

Rewriting: 1. Don't buy a car from that yard.
            5. If you want a cheap car buy it from a yard that sells them cheaply

It is a good idea to rephrase the conclusion like this so as to avoid silly complications about the relation between 5, which mentions you, and 1, which mentions me too.

How good are the inferences? The reasons for the conclusion sound quite convincing, but there are some reasonably likely counterexamples. For instance you might be such an expert on cars that even the most unscrupulous dealer in town is not going to fool you. Thus, the inference from 2 plus 3 to 1 is weak. The argument against the conclusion is much closer to being valid. I can think of no circumstances which are even remotely possible in which those reasons can be true and their conclusion - the opposite of 1 - can be false.

Overall, then, the reasons given against the conclusion are much more persuasive than the reasons given for it.

Exercise 908

1/Mary doesn't drink any more - not even beer/. 2/She joined the Baptists/ and 3/they make you sign the pledge/. Though from 4/the look of her nose/ I wouldn't mind betting 5/she still has the odd quiet one on the side/.

Clearly 4 needs rephrasing - her nose is red, or something like that.

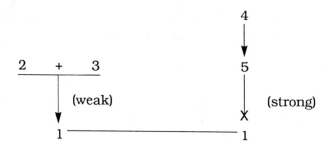

The inference from 5 against 1 is strong - so strong that you might have numbered 5 as "not-1". But the inference from 4 to 5 needs an extra reason - just what we cannot say, until we are told in what respect her nose looks like a drinker's nose.

The inference from 2 plus 3 to 1 is not as good as it looks. This is just like the Buddhist lady in an earlier exercise. Mary may have signed the "pledge", but what matters is whether she keeps to it. Until we are told that, we are not entitled to infer that she doesn't drink.

Exercise 909

I know that 1/you are working very hard at your logic, Tony/, but 2/you really do not have a chance of getting to the top/. 3/All of the great logicians have been women/.

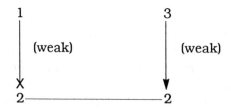

I prefer to diagram it this way rather than taking 1 as a reason for the opposite of 2 and 3 as a reason against that. But either diagram sets out the pattern clearly enough.

In assessing the inferences we have to be careful not to assume that some of the reasons which are not involved are true. In particular, when we assess the inference from 1 against 2 we must not just assume that 3 is true. Each inference must be treated on its own merits. Sure, in the passage the inference from 1 against 2 does not get a very good run for its money, but our job is to see whether it deserves better.

In this case, though, it does not come out very well even if we forget about 3. There are so many cases of people who have worked very hard indeed at logic but who have made little progress with it!

What about the other inference? If indeed all of the great logicians have been women, then so long as Tony is not a woman we might well conclude that he doesn't stand a chance. But we would be quite wrong to do that. There could be all sorts of reasons why the great logicians have all been women in the past which in no way prevent Tony from joining their ranks. That is, the fact that all As *have been* Bs is no reason at all for saying that all of them *will* be.

Overall, there is no strong argument here, either way. Both the reasons for the conclusion and the reasons against it fail to make anything like a convincing case.

Exercise 910

> I know that 1/May is a bad time to go up North for a holiday/, what with 2/the storms and most of the hotels being closed/, but 3/if you don't get away now you'll have a breakdown/. <So> 4/off you go!/

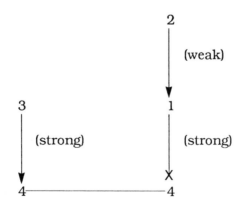

If you like a more complicated diagram you may break 2 into two. Anyway it should be rewritten as one or more statements: There are storms in May and most of the hotels are closed.

The inference from 3 to 4 looks good enough - or do we need to be told that breakdowns are to be avoided? However, what say you are going to have a breakdown anyway, whether you go away or not? Is that a counterexample? Think about it.

There are plenty of counterexamples to the inference from 2 to 1. That apart, is 1 a valid reason against 4? It is not easy to think of counterexamples this time, provided that it is May.

Exercise 911

> 1/Unless there is a major breakthrough in computer technology/ - and I must say that 2/on past performance the next one is already overdue/ - 3/you should stick with your old machine for a few years/ 4/The newer models don't have any important advantages over it/.

Restating 1: There will be no major breakthrough in computer technology.

I have opted for this bold move of splitting a conditional statement. This has the advantage of yielding a clear argument for a conclusion plus a reason against one of the reasons at least. I must admit that I am not at all sure that this is what the passage means, but if the passage is interpreted as I have marked it, the diagram goes like this:

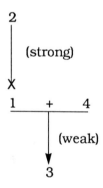

Briefly, the inference from 2 against 1 is a strong one, and the inference from 1 plus 4 to 3 sounds good, but there are plenty of counterexamples - you might get a real kick out of always having the latest-looking gear, you may want to impress everyone else, you may keep an ailing computer industry alive by buying new products even when they have no advantage over old ones. None of these is at all improbable, so the inference is actually a bad one.

Exercise 912

> When you are writing your essay remember that the people who mark it are ordinary human beings like you and me. If you are lucky you will get credit for what you have done, whether the marker agrees or not, but all too often they just look to see whether you are saying what they want you to say.

I am going to be bold with this one too, and declare that it does not contain any reasoning. Sure, we could add an unstated conclusion, but it would have to be something like "You should tell them what they want to hear" or "It doesn't much matter what you write". For one thing, neither of these follows from what is said. And for another thing, they are so different that I think we are wise to refuse to make any moves at all.

Even if I am wrong about this passage, there is a lesson to be learned. If we are expecting reasoning there is a good chance that we will find it whereever we look, whether it is really there or not!

Exercise 913

> 1 /It is a good idea to leave the catcher off the lawnmower/. 2/That way the clippings get left behind and they gradually break down and fertilise the lawn/. Granted, 3/they look untidy/, and 4/anyone walking inside will mess up the floors/, but 5/you will never have to put any of those chemicals on the lawn/.

This is a neat case where the reasons against the conclusion provide counter-examples to the argument for it, and the reasons for it in turn provide counter-examples to the argument against the conclusion.

Thus, since both reasons are likely enough, both inferences are weak.

Think about this for a moment. It is a good illustration of why the reasons for a conclusion have to be considerably more than 50% probable for the inference to be even moderately reliable.

Exercise 914

1/By far the best time to fish from the rocks is when the tide is rising/ 2/That's when the big ones come close inshore to feed/. Of course 3/ you're far more likely to be swept away by a wave than you would be on a falling tide/, but at least 4/if you survive you should catch plenty/

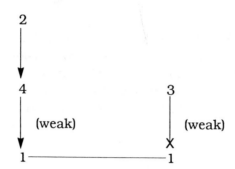

It is not clearly the case that 2 supports 4, so if you have linked them as reasons for 1 I will not argue with you.

What makes a time the "best" time to fish? The chances of catching fish? The chances of staying alive? This argument claims that you cannot have it both ways, and so in a sense is arguing that there is no best time to fish off the rocks. Of course if we were to restate the conclusion this way we would have to redraw the diagram, and there would be no reason against the new conclusion.

And the inferences? As it stands in the diagram, neither the inference supporting 1 nor the inference against it is a good one. But if as seems to be the case this is because 1 is ambiguous, probably we should opt for restating the conclusion and abandoning the use of "reasons against" in this example.

Exercise 915

1/All the experts say you should hold the bat straight when you are batting/, but 2/that way you can't get a good swing at the ball/. No, 3/unless you only want to survive for hours without scoring/ I reckon 4/you should just hold the bat naturally, keep your eye on the ball, and swing across the line as much as you like/.

Rewriting 3: You do not only want to survive for hours without scoring.

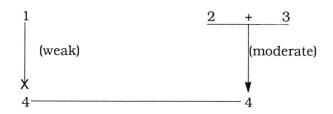

Note what I have done with the "unless" clause.

I see no advantage in splitting the conclusion into several statements.

If the experts really are experts then the inference from 1 against 4 has to be a good one. By definition, real experts know best. But clearly the passage is saying that the people who say to hold the bat straight are wrong, and so cannot be serious in calling them the experts. If then they are not experts, then the inference from 1 against 4 is a bad one, which suits the author of the passage just fine.

However, the inference from 2 and 3 for 1 is not much better. Even if the so-called experts are wrong, there are no doubt many possible ways of waving a bat at a ball, and only two have been mentioned so far. If some other way turns out the best, then we have a clear counterexample.

Exercise 916

> 1/Nobody is going to take you seriously as an artist unless you do "proper" paintings - big oils on stretched canvas/. I realise that 2/your best work is in the Japanese style - simple brushwork with black ink on paper/ - but 3/when people round here pay for a painting they want it to look expensive/. Sorry Edith, but 4/you have to cater for the market/.

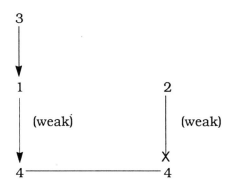

The structure of the argument is not entirely clear in the passage, so quite a range of diagrams is possible. And if 4 is the conclusion it is better to reword it: You have to paint big oils on stretched canvas.

The reasons in favour of 4 do not provide strong support unless we add the statement that she wants to sell her work. And the reason against 4 does not count strongly against it, unless we add the statement that she cannot work in both styles. In both cases the extra reasons needed are not obviously true, so we can reject the inferences as weak.

Exercise 917

> 1/The trouble with a daisy-wheel printer is that it cannot do italics or expanded type or graphics/. And 2/it is terribly slow - you even have to feed in sheets of paper one at a time!/ But 3/it produces much clearer copy than a dot-matrix printer, especially when you use carbon film ribbon/, and 4/that's important when you are trying to sell your work to a publisher/.

Unstated conclusion 5: Use a daisy-wheel printer.

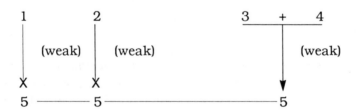

The two reasons against 5 strike me as independent of each other, so I have diagrammed them as convergent. The reasons for it are clearly linked.

How good are the inferences? Really, none of them is at all strong, because we are not told what is wanted, except that clarity matters in certain circumstances. We are not even told that these circumstances obtain; neither are we told whether italics etc are really needed nor whether speed is an important consideration. So, so far all of the inferences are poor ones. If we want to work out whether daisy-wheel printers are better than dot-matrix printers, or even which is better in which circumstances, we will have to find out a lot more. Hence it would be pointless to agonise over which case is stronger in the passage - the case for daisy-wheel printers or the case against them.

Exercise 918

I think 1/you should tell them what you think about it, Sue/. 2/Maybe they will treat you as a troublemaker/. 3/Maybe they will even turn nasty and fire you/. But 4/you have your self-respect to think of/.

It is hard to make any assessment of arguments like these. As they stand they are hopelessly weak. That is, without a context the reasons hardly support or count against the conclusion at all. But it is easy to think of contexts in which one or both of the inferences are quite good.

Exercise 919

1/By using artificial fertilisers the farmers here have managed to boost production by up to eighty percent in the last ten years/. 2/Without that, many of them would be out of business/. But 3/the runoff is killing the fish in the streams and lakes/, and 4/now there is so much weed growing in the nitrogen-rich waters that the whole drainage system is endangered/. Despite the benefits for production, 5/this use of artificial fertiliser will have to stop - immediately/.

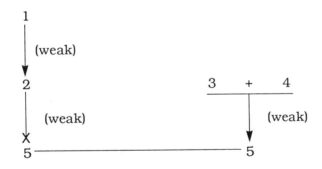

I have emphasised that I want you to concentrate on the strength of the inferences, and ignore the truth-values of the reasons. This exercise illustrates well the power of our methods. Although many people find the arguments here convincing, we can easily show that the inferences are very weak indeed.

Even the inference from 1 to 2 is not a good one, but it is not absolutely obvious that this structure is intended, as opposed to 1 plus 2 linking against 5, so we should not be too gleeful in pointing out the counterexamples this time. There are, of course, cases such as this: Production was quite adequate already and there was no threat of going out of business on that count, as opposed say to a lost market.

The inference from 2 against 5 is a weak one too. Counterexample: An initial use of artificial fertiliser kept the farmers in business but after that there was no further need for it or even advantage in using it. This may be a little improbable, but it is not highly unlikely and the argument does not rule it out.

And finally, the inference from 3 plus 4 to 5 is a weak one. It could be that the fish don't matter and the water weeds are easily eliminated and that the artificial fertiliser is absolutely essential for the farmers. A little unlikely again, but not highly unlikely.

Exercise 920

> Of course 1/it is hard to let them have their way when you think they are being short-sighted/, and of course 2/you will blame yourself for the rest of your days if it ends in disaster/, 3/as you are predicting/ But 4/<u>you have to let them make their own decisions</u>/. 5/They are not children any more/, and 6/if you try to force them they will probably move out of town/.

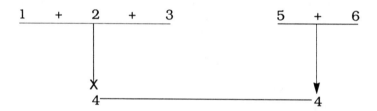

It is almost impossible to comment on an argument like this in isolation from any context. That is, whether the reasons for letting "them" make their own decisions are better than the reasons against depends crucially upon several unknown factors. In particular, does it matter whether "they" move out of town? If this is a bad thing the reasons for might be more compelling than the reasons against, but perhaps it is a good thing. Is it in any way relevant whether you may end up blaming yourself for some disaster? That depends upon how "you" relate to "them". In light of all the unknowns, we can do little more that point these matters out and leave it there.

The Acid
Test   10

Most of the passages used as exercises in this book have been made up specially for the purpose - a few have been borrowed from books and newspapers, but on the whole I have found it better to invent suitable exercises for each chapter.

The time comes though when this has to stop. The techniques you have been practising have to work on whatever you may come across "out there" in the real world. That is the acid test.

In this chapter you will have a chance to find out whether they do work. None of the exercises has been made up this time. They come from all manner of sources. Usually the source is not mentioned, being irrelevant to the merits of the reasoning. The exceptions are older passages, where the language can be rather out of date. In these cases I have indicated the source to warn you to be on the lookout.

As there are no new techniques involved in this chapter, we move straight on to the exercises. In my model answers I do not always use structure diagrams. I do not suggest that you follow this example, yet. Unless you are quite sure that you can test the major inferences for reliability without formally depicting the structure of the argument, use the full procedure.

EXERCISE TEN

Analyse the reasoning in the following passages.

Some passages will call for one sort of approach and others another. Choose with care.

You may have to reconstruct the argument - feel free to do this, restating the reasons and conclusions in your own words.

Explain your answer where necessary. In particular, use and refer to a diagram unless you can explain adequately without one.

1001 Fluoride in water [at the right concentration] substantially reduces dental caries. There is no evidence that it is associated with any harmful effects. Systemic supplements such as tablets have not been shown to be as effective. We have been well advised. Now it is up to each community to decide whether it will accept that advice.

1002 It is a crime for an individual to relieve himself or herself in a river; it is not a crime for a corporation to relieve itself in a river.

1003 Enter at once for the competition. If you win you get a handsome prize. If you don't you have the fun of competing. Either way you can't lose.

1004 A custom loathsome to the eye, harmful to the brain, dangerous to the lungs.... Herein is not only a great vanity, but a great contempt of God's good gifts, that the sweetness of man's breath, being a good gift of God, should be wilfully corrupted by this stinking smoke. (1604)

1005 You admit that my premises are true and my conclusion true. Yet you object that my argument is invalid. Aren't you interested in getting at the truth about this matter? And haven't I succeeded at getting at the truth?

1006 Smoking marijuana definitely leads to heroin use. A report by the U.S. Commissioner of Narcotics on a study of 2,213 hardcore narcotics addicts in the Lexington, Kentucky, Federal Hospital shows that 70.4 percent smoked marijuana before taking heroin.

1007 Any object begins to fall as soon as its support is removed. Hence a stone begins to fall as soon as it leaves the hand of the man who throws it. Therefore no stone can be thrown upward.

1008 No man will take counsel, but every man will take money; therefore money is better than counsel. (Swift - 1667-1745)

1009 A man who has no choice but to perform a certain action cannot be held responsible for it. A perfectly good man cannot help but behave well. Therefore a perfectly good man cannot be held responsible for his actions.

1010 Most New Zealanders live in a family, so it stands to reason most laws passed will affect the family unit.

1011 Robert the Bruce had the courage to show a defeated nation the road to freedom, but the Scots already believed themselves free, and this made it possible for Bruce to realise the national ambition.

1012 Consumption is the sole end purpose of all production; and the interest of the producer ought to be attended to only in so far as it may be necessary for promoting that of the consumer. (Adam Smith, 1723-1790)

1013 As any prison visitor knows, men convicted of rape and similar crimes usually admit to reading disgusting magazines and drinking alcohol before their escapades, and yet the authorities continue to turn a blind eye to filthy literature of all sorts, often with the pretence that it serves some artistic purpose.

1014 If you turn on the switch, then the light will go on; but if the light goes on, then the generator is working. So if you turn on the switch, then the generator is working.

1015 On Monday I got drunk on whisky and soda; on Tuesday I got drunk on bourbon and soda; On Wednesday I got drunk on brandy and soda; on Thursday I got drunk on rum and soda; I don't want to get drunk again, so no more soda for me!

1016 The silicon microchip would be extraordinary enough if it were only low-cost, compact electronics, but its ability to embody logic and memory also gives it the essence of human intellect. So, like the mind, the chip has virtually infinite application - and much the same potential to alter life fundamentally.

1017 Private industry has sufficient strength to develop without the assistance of government, and any government intervention would only hamper the development of industry. Because we are still in a recession, we cannot make our exports grow too rapidly. Under such circumstances, it is important for companies to build substantial strength within themselves. One of the best ways to do this is to promote research and development that will ensure future progress.

1018 According to Marxism, revolution is inevitable. One reason for this is the operation of "The Law of the Transformation of Quantity into Quality". All things change by imperceptible steps until there arrives a point, which Hegel calls the "node", beyond which a thing cannot vary while remaining the same. That this law exists can be seen when water turns to steam at 100 deg C and into ice at 0 deg C. This change occurs abruptly so that water is at one moment water and at the next moment steam or ice.

1019 You want to know if I think it's a good idea to take your cat camping? In a word, no. My long association with cats leads me to believe they are not generally good travellers and do much better left in familiar surroundings or even in a good boarding kennel. The stories of cats lost en route are legion. Their uncanny ability to escape almost any kind of restraint makes them poor risks for camping.

1020 The customary way to end this book is a strongly worded message to go out and put into practice all of the theory you have been learning. But as you know, such exhortations are always dubious and in the present case entirely useless. If you have studied the material properly you will aready know how to make use of the techniques of argument analysis and appraisal, out there in the real world, and so you will not need any final message from me. And if you have been less diligent you are unlikely to be reading these last pages of the book, and even if you are, you will be unable to do what I am supposed to be telling you to do. My final message to you should be: Go back to page one.

EXERCISE TEN - MODEL ANSWERS

As this book proceeds the idea of "model answers" gets less and less appropriate. Each exercise can be responded to in a variety of ways, and while some of these are much better than others, there can be several entirely good but radically different responses. The idea that any one response can serve as a "model" scarcely does justice to the complexity of the material and of the methods.

By now you do not need me to provide you with full answers. You will notice that there are not always diagrams in these model answers. Do not interpret this as meaning that I think you should be managing without them by now. If they help you at all, use them. Then if you manage to say what has to be said without referring to the diagram, it is all right to leave it out of your final presentation. That is what I have done here.

You will also notice that my answers are rather brief. You may prefer fuller answers, and in particular you may like to apply the formal techniques of argument appraisal more systematically.

Exercise 1001

1/Fluoride in water [at the right concentration] substantially reduces dental caries/. 2/There is no evidence that it is associated with any harmful effects/. 3/Systemic supplements such as tablets have not been shown to be as effective/. We have been well advised. Now it is up to each community to decide whether it will accept that advice.

Unstated conclusion 4: Water supplies should be fluoridised.

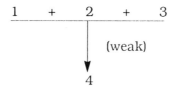

It is fair to state the conclusion unequivocally. Indeed this is little more than a restatement of parts of the last two sentences.

What else would we want to know, if we are expected to accept the conclusion? We would want to know (a) that there has been adequate research into harmful effects. There may be no evidence because there has been no investigation. We would also want to know (b) that we need to reduce dental caries. I do not mean that I have any doubts that they are undesirable, but if they are already at a very low level - and they might be - we may not need to reduce them. And we need to know (c) that the systemic supplements are not effective enough (they may be, while being less effective than something else). If these are added to the reasons stated, the inference becomes a strong one. But I do not think that we are entitled to add them, as they are quite likely to be false. So the inference is weak.

Exercise 1002

It is a crime for an individual to relieve himself or herself in a river; it is not a crime for a corporation to relieve itself in a river.

I think that we should come out fighting here and insist that this is a shabby argument. It might be a clever piece of propaganda, but as an argument it could be improved in several ways.

First, the conclusion should be stated since, although the author appears not to realise this, there are two equally apposite unstated conclusions here: that it should be a crime for a corporation to do this, or that it should not be a crime for an individual.

Second, the unstated reason should be written down. Of course once the conclusion is clear we know what has to be added. If as seems most reasonable the conclusion is that it should be a crime for corporations, we need to add the reason that whatever is a crime for an individual should also be a crime for a corporation.

And for that to be put into effect we would need some way of telling when corporations are "relieving themselves". I do not make this point as a clever objection against the argument. People I know who are into environmental matters usually have very clear ideas of what should be banned and why, not in terms of colourful phrases but in terms of exactly what chemicals have what effects upon what. The argument would be much better if this sort of detail were added. As an argument, that is. As a piece of persuasive writing it is probably better left alone.

Exercise 1003

> 1/Enter at once for the competition/. 2/If you win you get a handsome prize/. 3/If you don't you have the fun of competing/. Either way 4/you can't lose/.

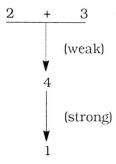

Do not look for anything subtle here - it is the sort of example you were handling with ease right back in the chapter on Meaning and Inference. The trouble with this one is that the word "lose" is ambiguous, and that this ambiguity is exploited. If you do not win the competition you do lose in one important sense - you do not get the handsome prize.

Exercise 1004

> A custom loathsome to the eye, harmful to the brain, dangerous to the lungs.... Herein is not only a great vanity, but a great contempt of God's good gifts, that the sweetness of man's breath, being a good gift of God, should be wilfully corrupted by this stinking smoke. (1604)

Note the date. I put it there to warn you to look out for archaic expressions.

Some reconstruction is called for. The conclusion is obviously some statement against smoking, but just what statement is not clear. That smoking is dangerous? That is it wrong? That it is wicked? Or what?

I am not going to decide. Maybe in 1604 people (King James actually) were clear what it means to say that something is "a great contempt of God's good gifts" but this means little to me.

So I am going to be a coward and say simply that this is an argument (if it is an argument) against smoking. And the reasons are: 1 It looks dreadful; 2 Is is bad for your brain; 3 It is bad for your lungs; 4 It makes your breath smell horrible. (No doubt there are others lurking in the language, too.) Unstated conclusion: 5 Don't smoke.

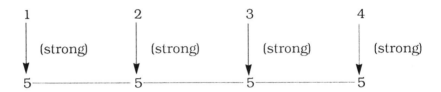

Are these compelling reasons against smoking? I must say that I find them independently sufficient. But a smoker might complain that there are reasons for smoking, and even that these outweigh the reasons against (surely there must be some rational smokers?)

My criticisms then are first that the passage is not clear (this is not its fault probably - no doubt the language was clear at the time - but still it is a fault); and second that it probably does not tell the whole story. (In fact I also believe that the argument makes use of some dubious quasi-theological notions, but as I have just been pretending not to understand them I should keep this remark firmly within parentheses.)

On the other hand it amazes me that the effect on the lungs in particular has been known for so long - or was King James just guessing?

Exercise 1005

> You admit that my premises are true and my conclusion true. Yet you object that my argument is invalid. Aren't you interested in getting at the truth about this matter? And haven't I succeeded at getting at the truth?

A formal analysis of this passage is not at all easy. Fortunately it is not at all appropriate either. What we need to do is discuss the issues rather than analyse the passage.

The question is: Is it reasonable to criticise an argument for being invalid when its reasons and conclusion are all true?

The answer is: Of course it is. We are interested not only in getting at the truth but also in how we get there. Anyone might get at the truth by sheer luck. If we already know what is the truth we scarcely need arguments at all, but if we do need arguments we need good ones. Invalid ones are no use at all, as they may lead us into error.

Exercise 1006

> Smoking marijuana definitely leads to heroin use. A report by the U.S. Commissioner of Narcotics on a study of 2,213 hardcore narcotics addicts in the Lexington, Kentucky, Federal Hospital shows that 70.4 percent smoked marijuana before taking heroin.

The conclusion is clearly stated in the first sentence, the reason in the second.

We all know what is wrong with this sort of argument. But while we all know what is wrong quite a few of us are not very good at saying what is wrong.

One way of saying what is wrong involves coming up with a spectacular counterexample. Like this: Suppose it is true that say 99.9 percent of the whole population regularly smokes marijuana (this is consistent with the truth of the reasons stated); then amongst the hardcore addicts the rate is lower than average, which suggests precisely the opposite of the conclusion (mistakenly) drawn from the data.

So what we need to know is what is the overall rate of marijuana smoking. We might say (if we are feeling charitable) that the argument assumes that the overall rate is significantly less than 70.4 percent.

That is one of the faults. The other main one is that, even if the overall rate is significantly less than 70.4 percent we want to know more before we conclude that marijuana leads to heroin. The other possibility is that some other factor is causing these people first to take marijuana and to take heroin and that this cause cannot be counteracted by preventing them from taking marijuana; indeed that might increase the heroin rate - they might go straight to heroin if marijuana is not available. Remember that even the possibility that this will happen counts against the argument.

So, even if the numbers are all above board, this is still a shabby argument. To establish a cause you must rule out coincidence.

Exercise 1007

> 1/Any object begins to fall as soon as its support is removed/. <Hence> 2/a stone begins to fall as soon as it leaves the hand of the man who throws it/. <Therefore> 3/<u>no stone can be thrown upward/</u>

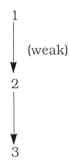

A straightforward ambiguity, cunningly exploited. In the sense in which the second reason is true, "fall" means accelerating towards the earth, and as any physicist will tell us, this does not mean moving towards the earth. Moving away at a decreasing velocity counts as "falling", here. So the velocity can be in any direction, not only downwards as stated in the conclusion.

The best plan is to insist on the everyday sense of "fall" rather than any unexplained scientific sense ("free fall"). Under this interpretation the inference from 1 to 2 is weak: 1 is true and 2 is false whenever something is thrown upwards, as this does not count as removing support. Thus, even if 1 is universally true, 2 is not and so we have no firm support for 3.

Exercise 1008

> No man will take counsel, but every man will take money; therefore money is better than counsel. (Swift - 1667-1745)

Those who know Swift will know to think carefully before responding. Indeed, even without knowing Swift it should be obvious that there is more than a little irony here. So one response is to say that it should not be construed as a straightforward argument at all, and in particular it should not be taken as trying to establish the "stated" conclusion on the basis of the two "stated" reasons. Rather, it should be taken as a nasty little criticism of the common practice of putting money before more important things.

Just how that argument works is not easy to spell out, nor is it easy to say how good Swift's argument is. As a first step we should perhaps reconstruct the intended argument:

> Counsel is better than money, and people should prefer what is better; therefore people should prefer counsel to money.

This is a deductively valid argument, and I think it is close to what the passage from Swift means, if we agree that it is ironical. So the argument gets top marks for validity.

Exercise 1009

> 1/A man who has no choice but to perform a certain action cannot be held responsible for it/. 2/A perfectly good man cannot help but behave well/. <Therefore> 3/a perfectly good man cannot be held responsible for his actions/.

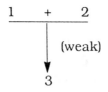

Arguments like this are rather common in Philosophy textbooks - from seemingly unexceptional reasons a counter-intuitive conclusion suddenly emerges. (If you haven't taken time out to work out what the conclusion means, start now.)

There is no standard good way of dealing with such arguments, but I suggest that we should be quite undaunted and apply to them the same common-sense tests we apply elsewhere.

In this case I would protest that we are supposed to accept that a person who cannot but do something has no choice. This is an unstated reason in the argument - without it the two reasons do not connect up at all. Now if I was to go into the truth of this unstated reason we would be delayed far too long, so for now all I will say is that it is not obvious to me that it is true and that anyone who wants me to accept it should take the trouble of persuading me. And I record the fact that I am not persuaded of the acceptability of the unstated reason by grading the inference as weak, provisionally.

Exercise 1010

> Most New Zealanders live in a family, so it stands to reason most laws passed will affect the family unit.

Some arguments are so bad it is hard to know what to say about them. This one actually appeared in a local news broadcast, and I should think that ninety-nine listeners out of a hundred saw nothing wrong with it.

To help them see, suppose we substitute "single storied house" for "family unit" - does the conclusion follow? No, of course it does not. There is no connection at all between the fact that most New Zealanders live in a certain sort of building and the nature of the laws passed. Or if there is, it is not this sort of connection.

The substitution is meant to draw attention to the unstated principle appealed to in the argument: that most laws will affect the way most people live (in a wide sense, although perhaps architectural details are not included). I have stated the principle as charitably as I can - a host of parodies come to mind - and even so it just is not true. Many laws passed are of a highly technical nature, often affecting very few persons in any direct way, and many others are very restricted in their application so that they will never impinge on most people.

Exercise 1011

> Robert the Bruce had the courage to show a defeated nation the road to freedom, but the Scots already believed themselves free, and this made it possible for Bruce to realise the national ambition.

Rewriting: 1. Robert the Bruce showed the Scots how to become free.
              2. The Scots were a defeated nation.
              3. The Scots didn't believe they were defeated - they thought they were free.
              4. (Therefore) Bruce was able to free them.

I will not swear that this reconstruction gets it right. For example the first statement in the passage might mean several things. I suspect that the reference to courage is a rhetorical flourish, but literally it could mean that when you try to tell the Scots they are wrong you had better look out for trouble. I doubt though that that is what is meant.

Anyway, this is not an entirely straightforward passage - it can be interpreted in several ways.

And it is not entirely clear what is being argued. The only explicit piece of reasoning is where 4 is inferred from 3. If the Scots hadn't believed they were free then Bruce would not have been able to free them.

I do not think that the usual methods work very well on this, because it is about how something which admittedly did happen could have happened. The best thing is to isolate the principle used in moving from 3 to 4 - You cannot free a people unless they already believe they are free. Stated baldly this looks wildly improbable. And perhaps that is all we have to say: that the only piece of argumentation clearly present in the passage makes use of a wildly implausible unstated reason.

Exercise 1012

> Consumption is the sole end purpose of all production; and the interest of the producer ought to be attended to only in so far as it may be necessary for promoting that of the consumer. (Adam Smith, 1723-1790)

There are only two statements here, and they are joined with the simple conjunction "and", so it seems that if there is any reasoning in the passage it is behind the scenes. (Unless we are meant to read "and" as "therefore".)

But imagine that Smith's statements were made in response to some view about the relative importance of the interests of consumers and the interests of producers. What do you think, from the passage, that that view would be? Surely, if Smith is trying to rebut any view, it is the view that the interests of producers are more important than those of consumers. So I am going to interpret the passage containing the unstated intermediate conclusion, that the interests of the consumers come first.

Reconstructing the argument:

1. The end and purpose of production is consumption.
2. Therefore the interests of the consumers come first.
3. Therefore the interests of the producers ought to be attended to only insofar as they promote those of the consumer.

To move validly from the stated reason 1 to the intermediate conclusion 2, Smith needs another reason, a general principle to the effect that if the end or purpose of A is B then the interests of those involved in B come before the interests of those involved in A.

Is that acceptable? One way to decide is to look for a counterexample. Let A

= general elections and let B = parliament. The end or purpose of a general election is to produce a parliament, but do the interests of those involved in the parliament - the successful politicians presumably - outweigh those of those involved in the election - the electors in particular? I do not think so, and for that reason reject the principle.

And does 3 follow from 2? Again I am sceptical, but this time I leave it to you to think of a counterexample.

Exercise 1013

> As any prison visitor knows, 1/men convicted of rape and similar crimes usually admit to reading disgusting magazines and drinking alcohol before their escapades/, and yet 2/the authorities continue to turn a blind eye to filthy literature of all sorts/, often with the pretence that 3/it serves some artistic purpose/.

Unstated intermediate conclusion:

> 4. Reading disgusting magazines and drinking alcohol causes people to commit rape and similar crimes.

Unstated final conclusion:

> 5. Reading disgusting magazines and drinking alcohol should be banned.

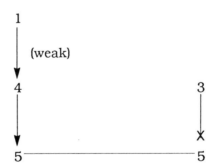

Inference from 1 to 4: We all know what is the basic thing wrong with this sort of argument - that correlation does not imply causation. And we all know to be wary of emotive expressions like "turn a blind eye" and "filthy literature". So we will have no difficulty in showing that the argumentation here is of a very low standard indeed.

I hope though that we will not stop there, even if we spend some time in establishing that this passage does indeed confuse mere correlation with causation, and does indeed indulge unfairly in emotive appeal (and you will have noticed that my remarks in fact do neither - I have said these, not shown them). It is not just of philosophical interest to wonder what you have as it were to add to a correlation to arrive at a case of causation. It is easy to be negative in this sort of case, but what would you do if you wanted to find out what is actually going on? Do you have any clear idea what you would do in this case? Given the correlation, what would you do to find out whether for example sexual offenders are actually effected by what they read and what they drink? And if they are, how they are?

And there is more to the argument that the question of what causes what. There is the question of what if anything should be done. The reasons for and against 5 should be discussed.

Exercise 1014

> 1/If you turn on the switch, then the light will go on/; but 2/if the light goes on, then the generator is working/. <So> 3/<u>if you turn on the switch, then the generator is working</u>/.

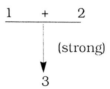

An occupational hazard, amongst logicians, is to seek mistakes in even the best examples of reasoning. So if you were sure in the back of your mind that there has to be something subtle amiss here, you were not alone.

But you were wrong. From the reasons "If p then q" and "If q then r" we are entitled to infer "If p then r".

If you want to know why, one way is to turn to the more formal branches of logic. Another is to work it out for yourself, as follows. "If p then q" means the same as "Not both p and not-q", so the two reasons tell us "Not both p and not-q" and "Not both q and not-r", which we can lump together as "Not p and not-q and q and not-r", and we already know "Not both not-q and q" (or "Not both q and not-q" if you prefer), which leaves us with "Not both p and not-r", or saying it the other way, "If p then r", which is the conclusion. So there is the conclusion, lurking there in amongst the reasons just waiting to be teased out of them. Which is why we are entitled to infer it. (If you like that sort of proof I think that you will enjoy Formal Logic. I do, and I do, anyway.)

Exercise 1015

1/On Monday I got drunk on whisky and soda; on Tuesday I got drunk on bourbon and soda; On Wednesday I got drunk on brandy and soda; on Thursday I got drunk on rum and soda/; 2/I don't want to get drunk again/, <so> 3/no more soda for me!/

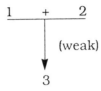

There is no point in dividing 1 any further.

Again we may laugh ourselves silly at the confusion between correlation and causation, but again we can learn something by asking just what else is needed if we are going to come up with good arguments of this type.

And it is not entirely silly to pick out the most obvious common factor as the causally relevant one. As a first move, subject to revision, it is entirely sensible. And it will only take Friday to rule it out if it does prove wrong.

So what this passage does is remind us that the most obvious common factor may not be the one that is doing the nasty work, that we may have to dig deeper.

I am not going to make the obvious remarks about just how to do that, here.

Exercise 1016

1/The silicon microchip would be extraordinary enough if it were only low-cost, compact electronics/, but 2/its ability to embody logic and memory also gives it the essence of human intellect/. <So>, like the mind, 3/the chip has virtually infinite application - and much the same potential to alter life fundamentally/.

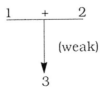

If we take away the word "essence" and talk instead about "some of the powers", the argument is no good at all. The fact that A has some of the powers of B is no reason for believing that it will have others. (Think of examples.)

So the word "essence" is essential, if the reasoning is to be any good. And if it means something like "the important powers", then perhaps the argument sounds rather better. But the same objection can be made - it can have some important powers of the human intellect and lack other powers.

Sometimes "essence" means "defining characteristics". Does that reading improve the argument? Well, if the characteristics mentioned in the final sentence are defining, it is getting better.

But are they? And is the ability to embody logic and memory a defining characteristic?

I have rather a "thing" about this word "essence". It has been used by a host of people, many of them philosophers, to do a host of jobs, and they do not always take the trouble to say what they mean by it. So do not be surprised if you find yourself going round in circles. I maintain that this is what will almost certainly happen if you throw around words like "essential" - in any metaphysically serious sense. So my complaint about the passage is not that the conclusion does not follow, but that the reason is unclear, using a word - "essential" - to which no single clear meaning is assigned. Tell me what you mean by "essential" and I will tell you whether the argument is a good one. In the meantime I am sceptical, and grade it as weak.

Exercise 1017

> Private industry has sufficient strength to develop without the assis-
> tance of government, and any government intervention would only
> hamper the development of industry. Because we are still in a
> recession, we cannot make our exports grow too rapidly. Under such
> circumstances, it is important for companies to build substantial
> strength within themselves. One of the best ways to do this is to
> promote research and development that will ensure future progress.

This is an argument against government intervention in industry. The main reasons are stated in the first sentence: It is unnecessary; It is harmful.

But that is only part of the picture. How do the other sentences link up with the theme of intervention?

The first one contains a chain argument: We are still in a recession; So we cannot make our exports grow too rapidly; So companies should build substantial strength within themselves.

Does this help the case against intervention? Maybe the idea is that this strengthening must be done by private companies themselves - that government intervention would hamper this.

And how does the last sentence fit in?

At this stage I think that we would be wise to use our analytical tools openly. This passage clearly has a rather complex structure of argumentation - exactly what our tricks work best on.

> 1/Private industry has sufficient strength to develop without the assistance of government/, and 2/any government intervention would only hamper the development of industry/. <Because> 3/we are still in a recession/, 4/we cannot make our exports grow too rapidly/. 5/ Under such circumstances, it is important for companies to build substantial strength within themselves/. One of the best ways to do this is to 6/promote research and development that will ensure future progress/.

What is the main conclusion? My guess is this:

Unstated conclusion 7: Government should not intervene in private industry.

If that is accepted (and I would not press the point) then the structure is something like this:

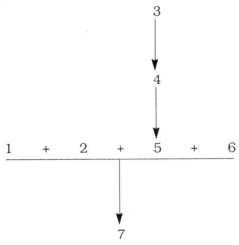

The crucial inference is the one to 7. Is it possible that all those reasons be true and 7 false? Do not be daunted by the weight of evidence. Rather, ask whether there are important considerations overlooked. And of course there are. The argument assumes that anything which assists in the development of private industry is a good thing. Once that is pointed out, we see how weak the inference is. For example, there is nothing in the argument to rule out the possibility that some very undesirable consequences will follow (eg massive unemployment, or poverty-level wage rates).

But I am not confident that this addresses the main point in the argument. This though is because I am not sure what that main point is, or even that there is one. Going back and reading the passage again, it seems to have two more or less independent lines of argumentation, one about intervention and one about research, and I am not at all sure that they are connected. I am not going to sort this out. The fault lies in the passage. It appears to contain a clear argument, but that is an illusion. On close examination it is not at all clear what conclusion is to be drawn, and in that case we can scarcely be blamed for failing to say anything useful about "the" argument.

Exercise 1018

> According to Marxism, 1/revolution is inevitable/. One reason for this is the operation of "The Law of the Transformation of Quantity into Quality". 2/All things change by imperceptible steps until there arrives a point, which Hegel calls the "node", beyond which a thing cannot vary while remaining the same/. That this law exists can be seen when 3/water turns to steam at 100 deg C and into ice at 0 deg C. This change occurs abruptly so that water is at one moment water and at the next moment steam or ice/.

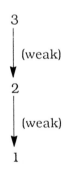

Even if the "proof" of the "Law" was in order (and clearly it is not, employing only one case to support a general proposition), it would not show that anything in particular is inevitable. It may be true that the Western economic system will arrive at a point beyond which it cannot vary while remaining the same, but unless what then happens is by definition a "revolution", the conclusion just does not follow.

Without knowing a lot about Marxism or Hegel, my guess here is that what happens is indeed defined by them as revolution, but if this is the case it still remains to be proven that it has the features that we would normally expect in a revolution, in the normal sense of the word. And the passage contains nothing to point towards that conclusion.

Exercise 1019

You want to know if I think it's a good idea to take your cat camping? In a word, 1/<u>no</u>/. My long association with cats leads me to believe 2/they are not generally good travellers and do much better left in familiar surroundings or even in a good boarding kennel/. 3/The stories of cats lost en route are legion/. 4/Their uncanny ability to escape almost any kind of restraint makes them poor risks for camping/.

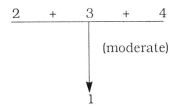

As far as it goes, this is not a bad argument, but does it cover all of the relevant considerations? I mean, we might grant that it is not a good idea to take the cat, but decide that it is an even worse idea to leave it behind. And while we might grant that there will be all sorts of difficulties, it could be further argued that they do not matter all that much. In particular, that although the cat is fairly sure to stray, it is also fairly sure to find its way home, eventually.

Not knowing a lot about cats I am not sure whether this is universally true, or true when great distances are involved. But I do know that it can happen, and therefore that the argument presented is not a compelling one. But assuming that it is about pet cats, and wanted ones at that, the inference is much better than many we have met.

Exercise 1020

The customary way to end this book is a strongly worded message to go out and put into practice all of the theory you have been learning. But as you know, such exhortations are always dubious and in the present case entirely useless. If you have studied the material properly you will already know how to make use of the techniques of argument analysis and appraisal, out there in the real world, and so you will not need any final message from me. And if you have been less diligent you are unlikely to be reading these last pages of the book, and even if you are, you will be unable to do what I am supposed to be telling you to do. My final message to you should be: Go back to page one.

As the passage says, either you can cope on your own, in which case you need no help from me, or you cannot, in which case it is unlikely that anything I can say will make any difference at this late stage.

About the Author

Born in Gore in 1941, the author grew up in Wellington, attended university there and in Christchurch, where he taught high school mathematics for five years and studied philosophy.

In 1969 he moved to the newly established Department of Philosophy at Massey University where he is currently a senior lecturer. Much of his effort has been devoted to developing extramural degree courses, notably in critical thinking. Currently his research is in the fields of aesthetics, philosophy of literature, and Maori ethics and metaphysics.

Married with three adult children, his leisure interests include writing and sailing. A volume of experimental poetry entitled *Can't Find Rest Room* is to be published in 1989.